A New History Of England, From The Earliest Period To The Present Time

Supported by

Liberty and Commerce.

Pub. July 20 1809, by I. Harris, Corner S.t Paul's Church Yard.

A NEW
HISTORY OF ENGLAND,

FROM THE
EARLIEST PERIOD
TO
THE PRESENT TIME.

ON A PLAN RECOMMENDED BY
THE EARL OF CHESTERFIELD.

By the Rev. Mr. COOPER,

Author of the Histories of ROME, GREECE, &c.

*By the Help of History, a young Man may, in some
Measure, acquire the Experience of Old Age.*
CHESTERFIELD.

THE SIXTEENTH EDITION,

CAREFULLY REVISED AND CORRECTED.

LONDON:

Printed for J. HARRIS, Corner of St. Paul's Church-
Yard; SCATCHERD and LETTERMAN, Ave-Maria-
Lane; LACKINGTON and Co. Finsbury-square;
DARTON and HARVEY, Gracechurch-street; and
B. CROSBY, Stationers' Court.

1812.

Price 2s. 6d.

Printed by E. Hemsted, Great New Street,
Gough Square.

PREFACE.

HISTORY, of all other studies, is the most necessary for a man who is to live in the world. It presents us with a review of all those mighty events which have influenced the fate of nations; and communicates to our inquiry the whole progress of improvement, the whole circle of knowledge and experience. In the delightful study of history we become acquainted with the characters, and even the persons of those heroes, who have triumphed over barbarity; of those legislators, who have strengthened the bands of society; and of those philosophers, who have instructed, polished, and reformed mankind.

In reading the transactions of others, we are apprised of our own duty; and the more we are informed of what is past, we shall be the better enabled to conduct ourselves for the future.

"The testimonies of ancient history," says lord Chesterfield, " are weaker " than those of modern, as all testimony

 " grows

" grows weaker and weaker, as it is
" more and more remote from us:
" but modern history, particularly that
" of the three last centuries, should be
" applied to with the greatest atten-
" tion and exactness; there the proba-
" bility of coming to the truth is much
" greater, the testimonies being more
" recent."

Such is the opinion of the Earl of
Chesterfield on the subject of history;
and fully convinced of the justness and
propriety of his observations, I have
followed his plan, as far as was consistent with the nature of this perform-
ance. I have, in the early periods of
English history, been as concise as possible: But, in the modern part, I have
been as copious and extensive as the
limits which I have prescribed myself
would allow.

INTRODUCTION.

THE ancient state of England with respect to its constitution, was originally a monarchy, under the primitive Britons : afterwards a province in subjection to the Romans : then an heptarchial government under the Saxons ; then a kingdom subordinate to the Danes ; next after them, under the power and dominion of the Normans ; but at present a monarchy again.

The whole island was at first called *Albion*, or *Alpion*, because the term *Alp* signifies a hill. It was likewise called *Olbion*, (a Greek word for happy) because the ancient Britons lived for a long time in ease and affluence, in the quiet possession of their hills, till the ambition of Julius Cæsar interrupted their flourishing state of peace and tranquillity.

It was afterwards named *Brithtania* from *Brith*, signifying painted in the

 British

British language, and the Greek term *Tania*, or country, which the Romans softened into *Britannia*.

Britain was but very little known to the rest of the world before the time of the Romans. The coasts opposite Gaul were frequented by merchants, who traded thither for such commodities as the natives were able to produce. These it is thought, after a time, took possession of all the maritime places where they had at first been permitted to reside. There, finding the country fertile, and commodiously situated for trade, they settled upon the sea-side, and introduced the practice of agriculture. But the inhabitants of the inland parts considered themselves as the lawful possessors of the soil; and sedulously avoided all correspondence with the new comers, whom they deemed intruders upon their property.

The inland inhabitants are represented as extremely numerous, living in cottages thatched with straw, and feeding large herds of cattle. They subsisted chiefly upon milk, and flesh procured by the chase. What cloaths they wore to cover any part of their bodies were usually

ally the skins of beasts; but much of their bodies, as the arms, legs, and thighs, was left naked, and those parts were painted blue. Their hair, which was generally yellow, flowed down upon their backs and shoulders. They constantly shaved their faces, except their upper lip, where they suffered the hair to grow to an enormous length. The dress of savage nations is every where almost the same, being calculated rather to inspire terror than to excite love or respect.

As to their government, it consisted of several small principalities, each under its respective leader. And this seems to have been the earliest mode of dominion with which mankind were acquainted, and may be deduced from the natural privileges of paternal authority. Upon great or uncommon dangers, a commander in chief was chosen by consent, in a general assembly; and to him was committed the care of the general interest, together with the power of making peace, and leading to war.

Their forces consisted chiefly of foot; and yet they could bring a considerable num-

number of horse into the field upon extraordinary occasions. They likewise used chariots in battle, which, with short scythes fastened to the ends of the axle-trees, spread devastation wheresoever they drove : while the warriors who conducted them darted their javelins with surprising dexterity, ran along the beam, leapt on the ground, resumed their seat, stopt, or turned their horses at full speed, and sometimes cunningly retreated, to draw the enemy into confusion.

The religion of the Britons was one of the most considerable parts of their government ; and the Druids, who were the guardians of it, possessed great authority among them. No species of superstition was ever more terrible than theirs ; besides the severe penalties which they were permitted to inflict in this world, they inculcated the doctrine of transmigration of souls, and thus extended their authority as far as the fears of their votaries. They sacrificed human victims, which they burned in large wicker idols, made so capacious as to contain a multitude of persons at once, who were thus consumed together

ther. To these rites, tending to impress ignorance with awe, they added the austerity of their manners, and the simplicity of their lives. They lived in woods, caves, and hollow trees ; acorns and berries constituted their general food, and their usual beverage was water. By these arts they were not only respected, but almost adored by the people.

It may be easily supposed, that the manners of the inhabitants took a tincture from the discipline of their teachers. Their lives were simple, but they were marked with cruelty and ferocity ; their courage was great, but neither dignified by mercy nor perseverance.

The Britons had long remained in this rude but independent state, when Cæsar, having overrun Gaul with his victories, determined upon the conquest of a country that seemed to promise an easy triumph. When the troops destined for the expedition were embarked, he set sail for Britain about midnight, and the next morning arrived on the coast near Dover, where he saw the rocks and cliffs covered with armed men to oppose his landing.

The

The Britons had chosen Cassivelaunus for their commander in chief : but the petty princes under his command, either desiring his station or suspecting his fidelity, threw off their allegiance. Some of them fled, with their forces, into the internal parts of the kingdom, others submitted to Cæsar ; till at length Cassivelaunus, himself, weakened by so many desertions, resolved upon making what terms he was able, while he yet had power to keep the field. The conditions offered by Cæsar, and accepted by him, were, that he should send to the continent double the number of hostages at first demanded, and that he should acknowledge subjection to the Romans. Cæsar, however, was obliged to return once more to compel the Britons to complete their stipulated treaty.

After the Romans had been in possession of this island nearly four hundred years, they left it to its ancient inhabitants again ; but as they were at that time most shamefully degenerated from their native courage and intrepidity, they were soon after invaded by the Scots and Picts ; and being greatly intimidated at the thoughts of their approach,

proach, they applied to the Saxons (through the plausible insinuations of their ambitious monarch Vortigern) for their assistance, and thereby brought on their total destruction, and the division of their country into the following heptarchy, viz. the kingdom of Kent, the kingdom of the South Saxons, the kingdom of the West Saxons, the kingdom of the East Saxons, the kingdom of Northumberland, the kingdom of the East Angles, and the kingdom of the Mercians.

In process of time, Britannia assumed the name of Angle-land, or England; and was successively governed by Egbert the Great; Ethelwolf; Ethelbald; Ethelbert; Etheldred I.; Alfred the Great; Edward the Elder; Athelstan; Edmund I.; Edred; Edwy or Edwin; Edgar the Pacific; Edward II.; Ethelred II.; Edmund, surnamed Ironside; Canute the Great; Harold I. surnamed Harefoot; Hardicanute; Edward the Confessor; and Harold, the son of Godwin, Earl of Kent. The pretensions of the latter, however, were opposed by William, Duke of Normandy, who claimed the English crown

crown as the lawful bequest of the Confessor. In the year 1066 he made a descent on the coast of Sussex, with a numerous army ; and soon after came to an engagement with Harold, who was defeated and slain at Hastings, as will be more particularly related in the account of the reign of William the Conqueror.

A New

A
NEW HISTORY
OF
ENGLAND.

WILLIAM I.

Surnamed the CONQUEROR.

WILLIAM I. king of England, and duke of Normandy, was one of the greatest generals of the eleventh century. He was born at Falaise, and was the natural son of Robert duke of Normandy, by Arlotte, a furrier's daughter. After the death of Robert, which happened in 1035, William, who was his only son, succeeded him. His relations, however, disputed the succession, but being favoured by Henry I. king of France, he triumphed over them, defeated count d'Arques, took Maine, and carried the war into Anjou. Some time after he paid a visit to Edward the Confessor, who treated him with great respect, and took a tour with him through England.

Edward

Edward the Confessor dying without issue in 1065, appointed him his heir; on which William sent to demand the crown; and soon after landed at Pevensey in Sussex, with a powerful army, and thence proceeding to Hastings, built a strong fort. Harold, the reigning prince, marched to oppose him, and a bloody battle ensued, the 14th of October, 1066, in which William obtained a complete victory, though he had three horses killed under him, and lost a great number of his troops; and Harold was slain with many of the nobility, and about 60,000 soldiers. Yet, notwithstanding this victory, William could have little hopes of gaining the throne by right of conquest; he therefore pretended that he came to revenge the death of prince Alfred, brother to king Edward; to restore Robert archbishop of Canterbury to his see; and to obtain the crown as his right, on account of its being bequeathed to him by Edward the Confessor. He cannot, therefore, be properly said to have obtained the crown by conquest, since these motives engaged many of the English in his favor.

William's passions were violent, but he had much wisdom, and an equal share of dissimulation. He marched directly to London; but on the way was met by a large body of Kentish men; each with a bough, or branch of a tree in his hand. This army was headed by Stigand, the archbishop, who

made

made a speech to the conqueror, in which he boldly demanded the preservation of their liberties; and let him know, that they were resolved rather to die than to part with their laws, and live in bondage.

William thought proper to grant their demands; he agreed to govern them by the laws of Edward the Confessor, and to suffer them to retain their ancient customs. Upon his coronation at Westminster, he was sworn to govern by the laws of the realm; and though he afterwards introduced some new forms, he preserved trials by juries and the borough law.

The first act of sovereignty he exercised, after his coronation, was the seizure of Harold's treasure, which he found amassed at Winchester. Part of this he distributed among the principal officers of his army; part was given to the churches and monasteries; and a large share was sent to the pope.

He began his reign with such moderation as afforded a happy omen to his subjects. He exhorted his principal officers to treat the English with humanity, and respect them as brothers. He issued orders throughout his army, forbidding his soldiers to attempt the chastity of the women, or commit the least outrage against the inhabitants, under the severest penalties. This specimen of his equity had a wonderful effect upon the English, who vied with each other in testi-

fying

fying their loyalty and esteem, by presenting him with large sums of money; which helped to defray the expence of the conquest; nor could they blame his conduct, when he divided among his followers the lands of all the noblemen who had appeared in arms against him.

He instituted the courts of chancery and exchequer; but at the same time disarmed his English subjects, and forbade their having any light in their houses after eight o'clock at night, when a bell was rung, called *curfew*, or *Coverfire*, at the sound of which all persons were obliged to put out their fires and candles. He repulsed several invasions, obliged the Scots to preserve the peace they had broken, compelled the Welsh to pay him tribute, refused to pay homage to the pope, built the Tower of London, and caused all public acts to be made in the Norman tongue. He likewise caused all England to be surveyed and rated, and had the men numbered, in a work called Doomsday-book, which is still extant.

He resolved to chastise the French, who invaded Normandy, and after that to reduce his son Robert; but Robert no sooner found that he was engaged with his father, than he dutifully submitted to him, notwithstanding his being victorious. Some time after, William declared war against Philip I. king of France; burnt Mantes, and ravaged the

country

country with fire and sword to the very gates
of Paris; but approaching too near the flames
of Mantes, the heat of the fire, together with
the warmth of the season, threw him into a
fever, which being increased by a fall from
his horse in his return to Roan, he died in
a village near that city, the 9th of September,
1087, in the 64th year of his age, after a
reign of fifty-two years in Normandy, and
twenty-one in England. He was interred at
Caen in Normandy.

William was a prince of great courage,
capacity, and ambition; he was politic,
cruel, vindictive, and rapacious; stern and
haughty in his deportment; reserved and
jealous in his disposition. He was fond of
glory, and, though parsimonious in domestic
affairs, delighted in pomp and ostentation.
His aspect was noble, severe, and imperious,
his stature tall and portly, his constitution
robust, and his strength so great, that few
men of that age could bend his bow, or han-
dle his arms.

Remarkable Events in this Reign.

1068. The English required to put out
their fire and candle at eight in the evening,
on the ringing of the curfew bell; and obliged
to deliver up their arms.

1072. Surnames first used in England,
and common swearing first introduced.

 1076. A

1076. A great earthquake in England, and a frost from the beginning of November to the April following.

1079. The courts of Exchequer and Chancery, the four terms of law, sheriffs, and justices of the peace ordained; and sealing of writs introduced.

WILLIAM II.

WILLIAM II. surnamed *Rufus*, or *Red*, from the colour of his hair, and his florid complexion, was the second surviving son of William the Conqueror, and succeeded his father the 27th of September, 1087. He was then thirty years of age; and at the same time Robert, his elder brother, succeeded, by his father's will, to the duchy of Normandy; but he resolved to assert his right of primogeniture to the crown of England; and several of the Norman nobility espoused his cause. William, however, defeated a body of his troops in Kent, and soon after prevailed on him to conclude a peace.

The two brothers then made war on Henry, their youngest brother, whom they besieged in Mount St. Michael, where the king riding one morning unattended, fell in with a party of Henry's soldiers, and endea-

voured

voured to force his way through them: but was dismounted, and a soldier was going to dispatch him, when he saved his life by exclaiming, " Hold, fellow, I am the king of England." Upon this the man dropped his sword, raised the monarch from the ground, and received from him the honour of knighthood.

The brothers being soon reconciled, William turned his arms against Scotland, and defeated the army of king Malcolm, who, with his son, had been killed just before in an ambush laid by Mowbray, governor of Northumberland. But Mowbray, finding, soon after, that the king neglected to reward his services, joined with other noblemen to set the crown on the head of Stephen, grandson to William the Conqueror. The king marched into Yorkshire, reduced Bamborough, took Mowbray prisoner, and put an end to the rebellion. But whilst he was hunting in the New Forest, he was accidentally wounded by an arrow, shot by Walter Tyrrel, his particular favourite, and immediately expired, on the 2d of August, 1100, aged 44, after a reign of thirteen years. It is said, so little respect was paid to his body, that it was conveyed in a coal-cart to Winchester, and was soon after interred, in a very private manner, in the church of St. Swithin.

William was equally void of learning, principle,

principle, and humanity; haughty, passion-
ate, brutal, profligate, and ungrateful; a
scoffer at religion, a scourge to the clergy;
vain-glorious, talkative, rapacious, lavish, and
dissolute, and an inveterate enemy to the
English, though he owed his crown to their
valour and fidelity, when the Norman lords
intended to expel him from the throne. He
lived in a scandalous commerce with prosti-
tutes, professing his contempt for marriage.
Having no legitimate issue, the crown de-
volved to his brother Henry.

William, at the time of his death, had the
archbishopric of Canterbury, the bishoprics
of Winchester and Salisbury, and twelve ab-
beys, in his hands; and in his reign he disposed of the bishoprics and monasteries to
those that bid most for them.

Remarkable Events in this Reign.

1088. A great scarcity, and the corn not
ripe till the end of November.

1091. Oct. 18. Five hundred houses in
London blown down by a tempest.

1092. A terrible fire in London, which
consumed a great part of it.

1096. The first decision by single combat.

1097. Westminster-Hall built by William
Rufus, 270 feet long, and 74 broad.

1100. An inundation of the sea which
overflowed the lands of Godwin earl of Kent,
to this day called *Godwin Sands.*

HENRY

HENRY I.

Surnamed BEAUCLERC.

HENRY I. surnamed *Beauclerc*, on account of his great learning, was the son of William the Conqueror, and the youngest brother of William Rufus and Robert. His engaging person and address, his courage, learning and eloquence, have been highly celebrated. Robert being in Palestine, when William Rufus was killed in 1100, Henry took advantage of his absence, and caused himself to be crowned king of England, on August 5th, 1100; but Robert, at his return, was acknowledged duke of Normandy, and landed at Portsmouth to make good his right to the crown of England. However, Henry came to an agreement with him, by consenting to pay him an annual tribute of 3000 marks.

This tribute, however, being but ill paid, they rekindled the war in a short time after; when Henry landed in Normandy, rendered himself master of that duchy, after the battle of Tinchebray, fought on the 27th of September, 1106, in which Robert was defeated and taken prisoner. After which Henry had the cruelty to cause his eyes to be put out, and confined him twenty years in Cardiff castle, in Glamorganshire. He died the 1st of December, 1135, aged 68, leaving

ing his crown to Maud or Matilda, his daughter, but was succeeded by Stephen, his nephew.

Henry was of a middle stature, and robust make, with dark brown hair, and blue serene eyes. He was facetious, fluent, and affable to his favourites. He had naturally a good capacity, which was so much improved and cultivated, that he acquired the surname of *Beauclerc* by his learning. He had great courage and fortitude, but was vindictive, cruel, rigid, and implacable. He was temperate in his diet, but a voluptuary in his amours, which produced a numerous family of illegitimate children. His Norman descent inspired him with a contempt for the English, whom he oppressed by extravagant exactions, which not only enabled him to maintain expensive wars upon the continent, but he died the richest prince in Europe.

Remarkable Events in this Reign.

1100. Henry I. restored to the English the liberty of using fire and candle by night.

1112. A plague in England.

1114. The Thames dry for three days.

1132. The order of knights templars founded.

1132. A great part of London destroyed by fire.

1134. A total eclipse, and an earthquake.

STEPHEN.

STEPHEN.

STEPHEN, surnamed *Blois*, was the son of Stephen earl of Blois by Adela, daughter of William the Conqueror, and succeeded his uncle, Henry I. the 22d of December, 1135, in the 31st year of his age, though the Empress Maud, daughter of Henry I. was then living. He endeavoured to strengthen himself against her, by taking a foreign army into pay, and by signing a charter, in which he acknowledged his being elected king by the clergy and people. He also confirmed the rights of the church, abolished the forest laws, and revived the favourite laws of Edward the Confessor; but not being able to reward the nobles according to their expectations, a war was soon raised against him, and he was obliged to conclude a disadvantageous peace with the inhabitants of Wales, and Scotland. He then fell ill of a lethargy, and the Normans, imagining that he was dead, invited Theobald, his elder brother, to seize his duchy: however, Stephen recovering, went over into Normandy, expelled his brother, and then returned to England, where the friends of Maud were ready to declare in her favour, assisted by the king of Scotland; but after the Scots had ravaged Northumberland, and the barons had fortified themselves in the southern counties, Stephen reduced the castles of the latter,

invaded

invaded Scotland, and compelled king David to conclude another peace with him.

He now wore the crown with great tranquillity for some time: but being jealous of the power of the clergy, he seized the castles belonging to the bishops of Salisbury, Lincoln, and Ely; upon which the bishop of Winchester, legate of England, and the king's own brother, became his most inveterate enemy. The clergy, who wanted not only castles, but garrisons, also made their ambition the cause of the people; and the Empress Maud took this opportunity of personally asserting her right to the throne.

The bowels of England were now torn by all the rage of civil war, while the people were plundered by both parties. The king faced the storm with a noble fortitude, he besieged the empress in Wallingford, pursued her to Lincoln, and gave battle to the earl of Gloucester before that city, when after a great effusion of blood, the earl was victorious: and the king having broken his battle-ax and sword in pieces by the force of his blows, was knocked down on his knees with a stone before he could be taken; after which he was confined in Bristol castle, and ignominiously loaded with irons.

While Stephen was in prison, the legate excommunicated his adherents; the duke of Anjou seized upon Normandy; and the sovereignty of Maud was every where acknowledged;

knowledged; but on her behaving with great haughtiness, and refusing to mitigate the severity of the Norman laws, a revolt ensued, and she was obliged to quit London. The legate, whom she had disobliged, now turning sides again, excommunicated her party, and Stephen being set at liberty, was every where successful, till the empress and her son Henry were obliged to retire to Normandy.

The young prince, soon after, landed an army in England, in order to obtain the crown, but in 1153 Stephen concluded a peace with him; and upon condition of enjoying the crown during his life, consented that Henry should succeed to it at his death. Stephen died the 25th of October, 1154, in the 50th year of his age, and the 19th of his reign.

Stephen was a prince of great courage, fortitude, and activity, and would have been beloved by his people, had he not been harassed by the efforts of a powerful competitor, which obliged him to take such measures for his safety as were inconsistent with the dictates of honour. His necessities compelled him to infringe the charter of privileges which he granted at his accession. His vices, as a king, seem to have been the effect of the troubles in which he was involved; for as a man, he was brave, open, and liberal; and during the short calm that succeeded the tempest of his reign, he travelled through

c

the

the kingdom, published an edict to restrain all rapine and violence, and disbanded the foreign mercenaries, who had preyed so long upon his people.

Remarkable Events in this Reign.

1136. A great fire in London, which destroyed a great part of the city, from Aldgate to St. Paul's church : London bridge, which was of timber, was also burnt.

The canon law first introduced into England, and appeals first made to the pope.

Eleven hundred and seventeen castles built by royal permission.

HENRY II.

HENRY II. son of Geoffrey Plantagenet, and the empress Maud, or Matilda, the daughter of Henry I. succeeded Stephen, the 20th of December, 1154, in the 23d year of his age. As the son of Geoffrey Plantagenet, he inherited the French provinces of Anjou, Touraine, and Maine, and afterwards, by his marriage with Eleanor, obtained Poitou, Saintonge, Guienne, and Gascony. In his person the Norman and Saxon blood were united, and in him began the race of the Plantagenets, which ended with Richard III.

In

In 1172, Henry sailed with a numerous fleet to Ireland, and landed at Waterford; all the Irish princes voluntarily swore allegiance to him, so that he became master of that kingdom without bloodshed, and divided great part of the country among the English nobles, who attended him in this expedition; and from them sprung some of the principal families now in Ireland. The king had for some years before met with continual disturbance, from the arrogance of Thomas Becket, whom he had raised from a mean station to the see of Canterbury; but at last four knights, thinking to please his majesty, murdered that insolent prelate. What is more extraordinary, the pope's legate prevailed on the king to do penance, by going barefoot to Becket's shrine, and to be scourged there by the Augustine monks, who gave him eighty lashes on his naked back.

Henry was brave, learned, prudent, polite, generous, and of a mild disposition; but these virtues could not exempt him from suffering the greatest vexations, even in his own family. Lust was his predominant passion; and Eleanor his queen, being jealous of Rosamond, (lord Clifford's daughter,) who was his mistress, and whom he kept at Woodstock in a labyrinth, built to secure her from the queen's rage, is said to have found means to dispatch her by poison; and the young princes, his sons, being joined by

several

several of the nobility, and assisted by the kings of France and Scotland, raised a great rebellion.

King Henry, however, took the king of Scotland prisoner, and afterwards not only restored the young princes to favour, but pardoned all the revolters; however, he obliged the king of Scotland to pay him homage for his kingdom. Henry was so mortified at the disobedience of his sons, that through grief he became ill at Chinon, in Touraine; and perceiving his end draw near, gave orders for his being carried into the church, where he expired before the altar, on the 6th of July, 1189, in the 57th year of his age, and the 35th of his reign. His ungrateful attendants stripped his body, and left it naked in the church; but it was afterwards interred at Fontevrand in Anjou.

Henry displayed all the abilities of a politician, all the sagacity of a legislator, and all the magnanimity of a hero. He was revered above all the princes of his time, and his death was deeply lamented by his subjects, whose happiness seems to have been the chief aim of all his endeavours. He enacted wholesome laws. He was generous even to admiration with regard to offences committed against himself, but he never forgave the injuries that were offered to his people.

He was of a middle stature, and an exact proportion;

proportion; his countenance was fair and ruddy; and his blue eyes were mild and engaging, except in a transport of passion, when they sparkled like lightning, to the terror of the beholders. He was broad chested, strong and muscular. He was eloquent, agreeable, and facetious; remarkably courteous and polite; compassionate to all in distress; and so charitable, that he constantly allotted one tenth of his household provisions for the poor. He also cultivated his talents, which were naturally good, and was a generous benefactor to learned men. He was, however prone to anger, transported with the lust of power, and, in particular, accused of incontinence, not only in the affair of Rosamond, but also in a supposed commerce with the French princess Adelias, who was bred in England, as the future wife of his son Richard. This breach of honour and hospitality is, if true, the foulest stain upon his character; though the fact is doubtful, and we hope the accusation is false.

Remarkable Events in this Reign.

1162. A sect called publicans, rejecting baptism, the eucharist, and marriage, came into England out of Germany, but the bishops pronounced them heretics, and they were burnt in the forehead and whipped.

1172. December 30, Becket murdered in the Cathedral of Canterbury by four knights.

 1176. The

1176. The kingdom first divided into six circuits, and three judges appointed for each circuit.

1177. The French king came in Pilgrimage to visit Thomas Becket's tomb.

1185. An earthquake overthrew the church of Lincoln and other churches; and at the same time there was almost a total eclipse of the sun.

RICHARD I.

RICHARD I. surnamed *Cœur de Lion*, or *Lion's Heart*, succeeded his father, Henry II. the 6th of July, 1189, at which time he was count of Poitou, and duke of Normandy. He commenced his reign by selling the crown lands, and exacting money on various pretences, in order to go to the holy war. He undertook this expedition in 1190, when he embarked with his whole army for France, where he joined the forces of the French king; and they having ratified their alliances, marched together with their combined forces, which consisted of 100,000 men, as far as Lyons, where they separated, and Richard continuing his march to Marseilles, reimbarked there for Sicily, where the two kings spent the winter; and the next spring, continuing their voyage,

Richard

Richard with his fleet was driven on shore
in the island of Cyprus, where Isaac, the
king of the island, treating the English with
inhumanity, Richard took him and his daughters prisoners; loaded the Cyprian monarch
with silver chains; and having thus conquered the isle of Cyprus, exchanged it with
Guy Lusignan, for the titular kingdom of
Jerusalem.

Richard afterwards gained a complete
victory over Saladin, took the city of Acre,
and made himself master of Ascalon, Joppa,
and Cæsarea; but being deserted by Philip
Augustus, king of France, and the dukes of
Burgundy and Austria, he could not continue
his conquests; therefore, on hearing that
his brother John was aspiring to the throne
of England, he concluded a truce of three
years with Saladin, and embarked in order
to return to his dominions: but having the
misfortune to be shipwrecked near Aquileia,
he resolved to pursue his journey in disguise
through Germany. After several difficulties,
he was taken, when asleep, in a mean lodg-
ing near Vienna, by order of Leopold, duke
of Austria, whom he had disobliged at the
siege of Acre; and that duke delivered him
up the following year to the Emperor Henry
VI. who, after treating him with great indignities, obliged him to pay 150,000 marks
for his ransom, which his loyal subjects
cheerfully raised by a voluntary tax.

He

He then returned to England, after an absence of four years, of which he had passed fifteen months in prison. He soon suppressed the party raised by his brother John, confiscated his lands, and then raising a numerous army, invaded France, and afterwards, at the battle of Blois, took all the archives of the kingdom, and continued the war against Philip, with various success, for five years, after which a truce was concluded. But a gentleman of Limosin having discovered a treasure upon his estate, Richard laid claim to it, as sovereign of Guienne; and besieging the gentleman in the castle of Chaluz, was wounded by an arrow on the shoulder, of which he died eleven days after, on the 6th of April, 1199.

Richard had a tall, graceful, fair, and well-proportioned person. His eyes were blue and sparkling, and his hair of a bright yellow, inclined to red.

He had prodigious strength of body, and amazing courage and intrepidity: his penetration was uncommon; he possessed a fund of manly eloquence; and was admired for his talent at repartee. He was an illustrious warrior, but exceedingly ambitious, proud, choleric, cruel, vindictive, debauched, and avaricious; and his love of glory made him neglect the happiness of his people. The reverend Mr. Grainger observes, that the saint-errantry of Richard, who sacrificed all

other

other views for the glory of the crusade, is an instance, among a thousand others, that offensive and enterprising valour may be a worse quality than cowardice itself; and that he was but eight months in his kingdom during a reign of ten years. He has been aptly compared to a lion, a species of animals which he resembled, not only in his courage, but likewise in his ferocity.

In this time the city of London began to assume a new form with respect to its government; to have a mayor, and to be divided into several corporations or societies, now termed companies.

Remarkable Events in this Reign.

1191. A total eclipse of the sun.

1192. Grain so scarce, that wheat was sold for twenty shillings per quarter, which was equal to six pounds of the present money.

1197. At this time lived Robin Hood and Little John; the former was betrayed at a nunnery at Berkley; being sick, he desired to be blooded, and was bled to death.

1197. A great famine throughout England, attended with a mortality.

Three lions passant, first borne on the royal shield of England.

JOHN.

JOHN.

JOHN, surnamed *Sans Terre*, or *Lackland*, was the fourth son of king Henry II. and was born at Oxford in 1166. He ascended the throne in 1199, after the death of his brother Richard I. though Arthur, duke of Brittany, to whom it lawfully belonged, as being the son of Geoffrey, his eldest brother, disputed it with him ; but the young prince being taken by surprise at Mirabeau in Brittany, in 1202, was murdered in prison. Upon this, Constance, the mother of Arthur, implored the assistance of Philip Augustus, king of France, who promised to strip him of all the lands he possessed in France; and Pope Innocent III. not only excommunicated him, but absolved all his subjects from their oath of allegiance.

At length the pope sent Pandulph his nuncio into England, who offered the king the pope's protection, on condition of his swearing to obey the pontiff, and to resign his crown to him. To this John consented, and repaired to Dover church, in the presence of the priests and people, took off his crown, disrobed himself, and laid all his ensigns of royalty at the feet of the nuncio, who was seated on a throne. After this, he signed a paper, by which he resigned the kingdom of England, with the lordship of

Ireland,

Ireland, to the holy see; and bound himself as a vassal, to pay 700 marks annually for England, and 300 for Ireland ; and then did homage to the pope in the person of his nuncio, who kept the crown and sceptre five days in his possession.

The barons of England, fired with indignation at this meanness, and oppressed by the heavy taxes with which he loaded them, had recourse to arms, and demanded a re-establishment of the laws of Edward the Confessor, and a renewal of the charter of Henry 1. which being refused by the king, they chose Robert Fitzwalter for their general; marched to London, and besieged him in the Tower. The king complied when he could no longer resist, and agreed to meet the barons in Runnymede, or the Mead of Counsel, between Staines and Windsor; and there, being unable to obtain supplies from his people, and finding himself too weak to withstand his enemies, granted whatever they desired; hence rose that famous charter of liberties, called *Magna Charta*, which he was obliged to sign, and also the charter of the liberties of the forest, charters that have since been esteemed the foundation of the English liberties.

The king, however, though he had ratified these charters with a most solemn oath, brought over an army from Flanders, and ravaged the whole kingdom. Upon this the

the barons applied for assistance to the king of France, promising the crown to his son Lewis, if he would come with a force sufficient to rescue them from the tyranny of John.

Lewis soon came to their assistance, landed at Sandwich, and took Rochester, while John retired to Winchester, having prevailed on the pope to excommunicate both the French king and the English barons; but being deserted by some of his mercenaries, the dauphin besieged Dover, while the barons invested Windsor; after which the country was ravaged by both parties, who came to no engagement. At length, grief and fatigue threw the king into a fever, which is said to have been heightened by his eating of peaches and drinking new ale. He died at Newark, October 18, 1216, in the 51st year of his age, and the 17th of his reign. Others say, that he was poisoned by a monk.

John was in his person taller than the middle size, of a good shape, and agreeable countenance. With respect to his disposition, it is strongly delineated in the transactions of his reign. If his understanding were contemptible, his heart was the object of detestation: we find him slothful, shallow, proud, imperious, sudden, rash, cruel, vindictive, perfidious, cowardly, libidinous, and inconstant; abject in adversity, and over-

bearing

bearing in success; contemned and hated by his subjects, over whom he tyrannized to the utmost of his power; abhorred by the clergy, whom he oppressed with exactions; and despised by all the neighbouring princes of Europe.

Though he might have passed through life without incurring such a load of odium and contempt, had not his reign been perplexed by the turbulence of his barons, the rapaciousness of the pope, and the ambition of such a monarch as Philip Augustus; his character would never have afforded one quality that would have exempted him from the disgust and scorn of his people. However, it must be acknowledged that his reign was not altogether barren of laudable transactions. He regulated the form of the civil government in the city of London, and several other places in the kingdom: he was the first who coined sterling money; introduced the laws of England into Ireland, and granted to the Cinque-ports those privileges of which they are still possessed.

Remarkable Events in this Reign.

1202. The assize of bread first appointed.

1212. Great part of London destroyed by fire; and near 3000 people perished by that accident.

London bridge built of stone, was finished.

Sterling

Sterling money first coined in England, and the Cinque-ports endowed with various privileges.

︎◌◌◌◌◌◌

HENRY III.

HENRY III. king of England, commonly called *Henry of Winchester*, was born October 1, 1207, and succeeded his father, king John, the 28th of October, 1216, when he was only nine years of age. Lewis, the dauphin of France, afterwards Lewis VII. who was called in by the barons against king John, was then in England; but having received a large sum of money, returned into France. When Henry came of age, he began by exacting large sums of money, and annulling the two sacred charters granted by his father. He landed in Brittany with a numerous army, in order to recover the British dominions in France; but, spending his time in diversions, he shamefully returned, after having spent all his treasures. Afterwards renewing the war, he lost all Poitou, and then concluded a peace with Lewis for five years, to purchase which, Henry agreed to pay him 5000 pounds annually.

The king paid no regard to the constitution of England, but he met with many mortifications

tifications from his parliament and people, .who at length obliged him to renew the two charters ; which was done in Westminster-hall in the following manner.—The peers being assembled in the presence of the king, each holding a lighted taper, the archbishop of Canterbury denounced a terrible curse against those who should violate the laws, or alter the constitutions of the kingdom : then the charters were read aloud, and confirmed by the king, who all this time kept his hand upon his breast : after which every one threw his taper on the ground, to raise a great smoke, and wished that those who violated the charters might smoke in hell. After this, the parliament granted him a subsidy for suppressing an insurrection in Guienne. He soon reduced that province, and returned to England, where he renewed his exactions.

The people being still oppressed, and the barons finding that Henry could not be bound by the most solemn oaths, undertook to reform the government; accordingly, commissioners were chosen by the king and the barons, and articles agreed on, which the king again broke. At last they came to an open war, when a decisive battle was fought near Lewes, in Sussex, in which the king's army was defeated, and himself, prince Edward, and the king of the Romans, taken prisoners. But afterwards the earls of Leicester and Gloucester quarrelling, the latter

joined

joined prince Edward, who had escaped
from his keepers, and uniting their forces,
marched against the earl of Leicester, whom
they defeated and slew. The king was then
set at liberty, but peace was not restored till
some time after; when prince Edward engaged in a crusade, and went to the Holy
Land. His father, king Henry, did not live
to see him return, but died at London, on
the 16th of November, 1272, aged 65, in
the 56th year of his reign, and was buried in
Westminster-abbey. He had nine children,
of whom only two sons, Edward and Edmund, and two daughters, Margaret and
Beatrix, survived him.

Henry was of a middle size, and robust
make, and his countenance had a peculiar
cast from his left eye-lid, which hung down
so far as to cover part of his eye. He was a
prince of very mean talents; irresolute, inconstant, and capricious; proud, insolent,
and arbitrary; arrogant in prosperity, and
abject in adversity; profuse, rapacious, and
choleric, though destitute of liberality, economy, and courage. Yet his continence was
praise-worthy, as well as his aversion to
cruelty; for he contented himself with punish-
ing the rebels in their effects, when he might
have glutted his revenge with their blood.
He was prodigal even to excess, and therefore always in necessity. Notwithstanding
the great sums he levied from his subjects,
and

and though his occasions were extremely pressing, he could not help squandering away his money upon worthless favourites, without considering the difficulty he always found in obtaining supplies from parliament.

Remarkable Events in this Reign.

1217. The orders of Franciscans and Dominicans settled in England.

1218. St. Peter's house in Cambridge founded by Hugh de Balsam, tenth bishop of Ely.

1220. Thomas a Becket's bones enshrined in gold, and set with precious stones by the then archbishop.

1221. The first stone of Westminster abbey laid.

1222. Three impostors, one of whom pretended to be Jesus Christ, were sentenced to perpetual imprisonment, and to be fed on bread and water.

1223. A synod held, which forbad the marriage of priests.

1225. Two notable impostors executed, one for pretending to be the Virgin Mary, and the other Mary Magdalen.

1242. Aldermen first elected in London.

1246. Tiles first brought in use.

1251. Wales wholly subdued, and governed by the English laws.

1251. Magna Charta solemnly confirmed.

 1253.

1253.　Fine linen first made in England.

1269.　The bones of Edward the Confessor enshrined in gold, and set with precious stones.

EDWARD I.

EDWARD I. king of England, surnamed *Long-shanks*, was the son of Henry III. and born at Winchester, June 16, 1230. He carried on a crusade against the Saracens, where with only 10,000 Englishmen, he struck a general panic into the infidels. He there narrowly escaped destruction, being wounded by an assassin in the arm with a poisoned dagger; and it is said that he owed his life to the affection of his queen Eleanor, who sucked the venom out of the wound. While he was on his return from Palestine, he heard of the death of his father, which happened in 1272; and arriving in England with his queen, they were both crowned on the 9th of August, 1274. He began his reign by confirming the Magna Charta, and by making a strict enquiry into the affairs of the kingdom. He then defeated and slew Lewellin prince of Wales, who had revolted; and afterwards summoning a parliament at Ruthen, it was there resolved that Wales should be united to England: when some of the Welsh nobles telling the king,

king, that he would never peaceably enjoy their country, till they were governed by a prince of their own nation, he sent for the queen to lie-in at Caernarvon, where being delivered of a prince, the states acknowledged him for their sovereign ; and, since that time, the eldest sons of the kings of England have borne the title of Prince of Wales. Soon after, queen Eleanor dying at Grantham, in Lincolnshire, Edward erected a cross at every place where the corpse rested in the way to Westminster.

Edward then carrying his arms into Scotland, took Berwick, Dunbar, and Edinburgh ; and John Baliol, their king, repairing to Edward, renewed his oath of fidelity, and put the whole kingdom in his power. But while Edward was endeavouring to recover some dominions which he had lost in France by treachery, the brave William Wallace rose up in the defence of his country, and having suddenly dispossessed the English of all the strong places they held, was declared regent of the kingdom : on which Edward hastily returned from France, advanced into Scotland at the head of a powerful army, and defeated Wallace, who, several years after, was betrayed into the hands of the English, and sent to London, where that great hero suffered the death of a traitor. Edward was seized with a dysentery, and died at a place called Burgh on the

Sands,

Sands, in Cumberland, on July 7, 1307, in the 68th year of his age, and the 35th of his reign, and was interred in Westminster-abbey. He was a prince of a very dignified appearance, tall in stature, regular and comely in his features, with keen piercing black eyes, and of an aspect that commanded reverence and esteem. His constitution was robust; his strength and dexterity perhaps unequalled in his kingdom; and his shape was unblemished in all other respects but that of his legs, which are said to have been too long in proportion to his body; whence he derived the epithet of Long Shanks. In the qualities of the head, he equalled the greatest monarchs who have sat on the English throne; he was cool, pene-trating, sagacious, and circumspect. The remotest corners of the earth resounded with the fame of his courage; and all over Europe he was considered as the flower of chivalry. Nor was he less consummate in his legislative capacity than eminent for his military prowess. He new modelled the administration of justice, so as to render it more sure and summary; he fixed proper bounds to the different courts of jurisdiction; settled a new and easy method of collecting the revenue, and established wise and ef-fectual regulations for preserving peace and order among his subjects. Yet, with all these good qualities, he cherished a danger-

ous

ous ambition, to which he did not scruple to sacrifice the good of his country. That he was arbitrary in his disposition, appears in many instances of his reign, particularly that of seizing for his own use the merchandise of his subjects. The cruelty of his nature was manifested in every expedition he undertook either in Wales or Scotland. Though he is celebrated for his chastity and regular deportment, there is not, in the whole course of his reign, one instance of liberality or munificence. He had great abilities, but no genius; and was an accomplished warrior, without the least spark of heroism.

Remarkable Events in this Reign.

1279. Two hundred and eighty Jews hanged for clipping and coining.

1285. Westminster-abbey finished sixty years after it was founded.

1286. All Jews seized by order of the king, and twelve thousand pounds of silver extorted from them.

1299. Spectacles first invented by a monk of Pisa.

1302. The magnetic needle first brought into use.

EDWARD II.

Surnamed of CAERNARVON.

EDWARD II. king of England, was born at Caernarvon, April 25, 1284, and succeeded his father, Edward I. in 1307, at 23 years of age. He recalled Piers Gaveston, the debaucher of his youth, whom his father had banished. Then marrying Isabella of France, the daughter of Philip the Fair, they were both crowned at Westminster, on the 24th of February, 1308. His ridiculous fondness for Gaveston occasioned innumerable disputes, till at length the barons had recourse to arms, and Gaveston was beheaded. An accommodation was afterwards effected between the king and the barons, and peace restored in 1312. The same year the queen was delivered of a son, who was named Edward. In the mean time, the Scots obtained three victories over the English, and made themselves masters of every place in Scotland. This weak prince raised the two Spencers, father and son, to the summit of power; who being banished by the parliament, the king levied an army, took some castles from the barons, and recalled his two favorites.

Some time after, Edward invaded Scotland; but wanting provisions, he returned without striking a blow; on which Bruce,

king

king of Scotland, pursued him to York, and after having destroyed twenty thousand of the English, consented to a peace for thirteen years. The two Spencers soon incurred the general hatred, and queen Isabella flying to France with her son, the nobility sent for her; when landing, and proceeding toward London with a numerous army, the king fled into the west; she still pursued him, and he set sail for Ireland, but was driven back into Wales, and being taken, was sent prisoner to the queen. Hugh Spencer, the father, was hanged and quartered without a trial, and the young Spencer was hanged on a gibbet 50 feet high.

The queen was entirely governed by Roger Mortimer, earl of March, whom she took to her bed: and the king being obliged to resign the crown in 1327, his son Edward was proclaimed king. After these transactions, the late sovereign was treated with the greatest indignities, and at last inhumanly murdered in Berkley-castle; for some assassins having covered him with a feather-bed, held him down, while others conveyed a horn pipe up his body, through which they thrust a red hot iron, and thus burnt his bowels. His body was buried in a private manner in the abbey church at Gloucester, and it was given out that he died a natural death.

Thus perished Edward II. after having atoned by his sufferings for all the errors of his conduct.

conduct. He resembled his father in the accomplishments of his person, as well as in his countenance; but in other respects he seems to have inherited only the defects of his character; for he was cruel and illiberal, without his valour or capacity. He had levity, indolence, and irresolution, in common with other weak princes: but the distinguishable foible of his character was that unaccountable passion for the reigning favorite, to which he sacrificed every other consideration of policy and convenience, and at last fell a miserable victim. Yet his bitterest enemies never alledged that any thing unnatural entered into the composition of that singular attachment which he expressed for Gaveston and the younger Spencer. In this reign there was the most terrible earthquake that had ever been felt in England, and a dreadful famine, which lasted three years, and destroyed a vast number of people.

Remarkable Events in this Reign.

1309. Crockery-ware invented.

1316. Exeter College, Oxford, founded by Walter Stapleton, bishop of Exeter.

1316. On account of a great famine this year the parliament limited the price of provisions as follows; an ox for sixteen shillings; a cow, twelve shillings; a hog, two years old, three and four-pence; a sheep unshorn, one shilling and eight-pence; if shorn, one shilling and

and two-pence; a goose, two-pence-half-penny; a capon, two-pence; a hen, one penny; twenty-four eggs, one penny; a quarter of wheat, beans, or pease, sold for twenty shillings; and whoever did not comply with this regulation, forfeited the provisions to the king.

1319. The university of Dublin founded.

1322. The order of the Knights Templars abolished by Pope Clement the First.

1326. Oriel college in Oxford founded by the king, or his almoner, Adam de Blome.

EDWARD III.

EDWARD III. was born at Windsor, November 15, 1312, and was placed on the throne the 26th day of January, 1327, at 14 years of age, while his father Edward II. was living. Though a regency was appointed by the parliament, the queen and Roger Mortimer had the sole authority; and, influenced by them, the young king not only renounced all pretensions to Scotland, but gave his sister in marriage to David Bruce king of the Scots; yet, afterwards becoming sensible of the queen's ill conduct, he confined her for life, and caused Mortimer earl of March to be hanged at Tyburn. He then broke the truce with Scotland, invaded that kingdom, and obliged king David to fly with

his

his queen into France, when he set up Edward Baliol, son of John Baliol, in his room. The king of England marched an army to lay siege to Berwick, which was still in king David's hands. The regent of Scotland advanced with a great army to its relief, but Edward met him at Hallidown-hill, and in a bloody battle, A. D. 1333, entirely routed him, after which Berwick surrendered, and was annexed for ever to the crown of England. However, the Scots drove Baliol out of the kingdom; upon which Edward marched with a numerous army in 1335, and attacked Scotland by sea and land, whereupon they submitted. Edward now laid claim to France; for Charles, his mother's brother, dying, Philip of Valois had possessed himself of the kingdom, alledging the Salic Law; but Edward asserted, that the Salic Law, in excluding females from the succession, did not exclude their male issue: on which he grounded his title. His first campaign passed without bloodshed, but he took the title of king of France, and quartered his arms with the fleurs de lis, adding the motto *Dieu et mon droit*, or, God and my right. However, in his next attempt, he defeated the French fleet. He then besieged Tournay; but being called home to oppose the Scots, concluded a truce for one year with Philip king of France. In the next campaign he ravaged all the country up to the walls of Paris, and

his

his son the Black Prince of Wales, at sixteen years of age, won the glorious battle of Cressy. Six weeks after this, queen Philippa defeat-ed the Scots, and took king David prisoner. These memorable victories were obtained in 1346. Edward then laid siege to Calais, and having reduced it by famine, returned to England. He soon after sent the Black Prince, who, after taking several towns, to-tally routed the French army, commanded by king John, who had succeeded Philip ; and in this memorable battle, which was fought near Poictiers, took the king, many nobles, and a multitude of private men prisoners, though the French army was six times as nu-merous as the English. Thus Edward had the honour of having two kings his prisoners at the same time, John of France, and David Bruce king of Scotland. The king of Scot-land, who resided at Odiham, in Hampshire, was afterwards ransomed for 100,000 marks ; and the French king, who lived at the Savoy, agreed to give for his ransom 500,000 pounds, and a considerable extent of country.

Charles king of France afterwards carried on a war with Edward, when the English were driven from all the places they had so nobly conquered, except Calais. However, a truce was concluded between the two crowns in 1374.

On June 8, 1376, died Edward prince of Wales, the delight of the nation, in the 46th

year of his age. He was called the Black
Prince, from wearing black armour. The
parliament attended his corpse to Canterbury, where he was interred.

King Edward distinguished himself by in-
stituting the order of the garter; and died at
Richmond in Surrey, June 21, 1377, in the
65th year of his age, and the 51st of his reign,
and was interred in Westminster-abbey.

Edward III. was, doubtless, one of the
greatest princes that ever swayed the sceptre
of England, whether we consider him as a
warrior or a lawgiver, a monarch or a man.
He was tall, majestic and finely shaped, with
a piercing eye, and aquiline visage. He excelled all his contemporaries in feats of arms,
or personal address. He was courteous, affable, and eloquent, of a free deportment,
and agreeable conversation, and had the art
of commanding the affection of his subjects,
without seeming to solicit popularity. He
was a constitutional knight-errant, and his example diffused the spirit of chivalry through
the whole nation. The love of glory was
certainly the predominant passion of Edward,
to the gratification of which he did not scruple
to sacrifice the feelings of humanity, the lives
of his subjects, and the interest of his country. And nothing could have induced or enabled his people to bear the load of taxes
with which they were incumbered in this
reign, but the love and admiration of his person,

son, the fame of his victories, and the excellent laws and regulations which the parliaments enacted with his advice and concurrence.

Remarkable Events in this Reign.

1330. Gunpowder invented by Swarth, a monk of Cologne.

1331. The art of weaving silk brought from Flanders to England by John Kemp.

1340. Edward took the title of *King of France,* and quartered with his own arms the fleur de lis of France. At the same time he used the motto, *Dieu et mon droit.*

1344. Gold first coined in England.

1346. Cannon first used by the English at the battle of Cressy.

1352. At this time the largest silver coin in England was a groat.

1361. A great plague in England, which, between January and July, took off in London 57,374 persons.

1362. An act made, that the council should plead in the English language, French having been used before that time.

1362. A general pardon granted by the king for all offences.

RICHARD II.

RICHARD II. king of England, was the son of Edward the Black Prince, and was born at Bourdeaux, January 6, 1366. He succeeded his grandfather, Edward III. the 21st of June, 1377, at eleven years of age; when the parliament appointed several governors to the king, and ordered that his three uncles, with some of the nobility, should be regents of the kingdom. A truce which had been agreed to with France, being now expired, the French sent a fleet to ravage the coasts of England, and the regents ordered out a fleet to oppose them. The king of France also prevailed on Robert II. king of Scotland, to invade England; but the French king dying, the military preparations were suspended. In 1380, a poll tax being raised on all persons above 15 years of age, for the assistance of Ferdinand king of Portugal, against John king of Castile, it was levied with the greatest rigour and brutality by the collectors, on which a rebellion was raised, and 100,000 men appeared in arms, headed by Wat Tyler, a tiler of Deptford, and Jack Straw, who committed innumerable disorders, and entered London without opposition; but William Walworth, the mayor, killed Wat Tyler with a blow of his sword, and this great army was easily dispersed.

persed. The kingdom soon after becoming greatly exasperated at the ridiculous fondness shewn by the king for his new favorites, Robert de Vere, earl of Oxford, and Michael de la Pole, a merchant's son whom he had created earl of Suffolk, the parliament refused to grant the supplies unless he dismissed them from his service. But though the king said, " that to please the parliament he would not turn out the meanest scullion in his kitchen," and sent his chancellor to order them to grant the desired subsidy, he was obliged to part with his favorites, and to admit of fourteen commissioners to take care of the public affairs jointly with himself. The parliament were, however, no sooner dissolved, than they were recalled, and the king sent orders to the sheriffs, to let no representatives be chosen but what were in his list. He also endeavoured to raise an army to chastise his uncle, the duke of Gloucester, and the earls of Arundel, Warwick, Derby, and Nottingham, who were enemies to his favorites, and were considered as the protectors of the people ; but these lords speedily levying forces, defeated the earl of Oxford, who had been made duke of Ireland ; when the king took refuge in the Tower, where the next year, he answered the complaints of the lords with a shower of tears ; consented to the banishment of his favorites, who were accordingly sent into exile, and

.repeated

repeated his coronation oath. In 1392, the Londoners refusing to lend the king a sum of money, he took away their charter, and removed the courts of justice to York. Anne of Luxemburgh, the emperor's daughter, and the king's first wife, dying in 1394, he, in 1396, married Isabella, the daughter of Charles VI. king of France, who was only seven years of age, when a truce was concluded for twenty-eight years. Richard, however, extorted money from his subjects, and for inconsiderable sums, yielded Cherbourg to the king of Navarre, and Brest to the duke of Britanny. He ordered the duke of Gloucester to be seized and conveyed to Calais, where he was privately strangled, and some of the nobility were beheaded, and others banished. The Scots ravaged the borders of England, the Irish revolted, and the merchant ships were plundered with impunity by the corsairs of Holland. Seventeen counties were condemned as guilty of treason, and the estates of all the inhabitants were adjudged to the king, for granting assistance to the duke of Gloucester; but whilst he was employed against the malcontents in Ireland, a rebellion was raised in his absence, and at his return he was obliged to shut himself up in Conway castle in Wales. He soon after submitted to Henry duke of Lancaster, and was sent to the Tower; when a parliament being called, he was solemnly

lemnly deposed, and Henry proclaimed king, on the 30th of September, 1399 ; after which Richard was removed to Pontefract castle, in Yorkshire ; but on the 14th of February, 1400, Sir Pierce Exton, with eight ruffians, undertook to murder him, hoping thereby to please king Henry IV. and rushed into the room where he was, when Richard bravely wrested a pole-ax from one of the assassins with which he slew four of them ; but, Exton mounting on a chair behind him, struck him on the head with such violence, that he dropped down dead, in the 33d year of his age, after a reign of twenty-two years, and was interred at King's Langley in Hertfordshire ; but his body was afterwards removed to Westminster abbey by order of Henry V.

Richard II. had a very graceful person, and was of a sprightly disposition. He was, however, a weak, vain, frivolous, and inconstant prince ; a dupe to flattery, and a slave to ostentation. He was idle, profuse, and profligate ; and though brave by starts, naturally pusillanimous and irresolute. His pride and resentment prompted him to cruelty and breach of faith, while his necessities obliged him to fleece his people, and degrade the dignity of his character and station. He had no issue by either of his two marriages.

Remarkable

Remarkable Events in this Reign.

1378. A fleet fitted out at the private expence of an alderman, and a great number of prizes taken.

1378. Greenland discovered by a Venetian.

1381. Bills of exchange first used in England.

1387. The first high admiral of England.

1338. Bombs invented by a man at Venlo.

1391. Playing cards invented for the amusement of the king of France.

1398. Cheshire erected into a principality.

In this reign also the ladies wore high dresses on their heads, piked horns, with long-trained gowns, and rode on side saddles, after the example of the princess Anne of Bohemia, who first brought that fashion into this country, before which time they used to ride astride like men.

HENRY IV.

Surnamed of BOLINGBROKE.

HENRY IV. duke of Lancaster and Hereford, was born in 1367, and proclaimed king after the deposition of Richard II. on the 30th of September, 1399. He was the eldest son of John of Gaunt, duke

of

of Lancaster, third son of Edward III. He had not a just claim to the crown, which of right belonged to Edward Mortimer earl of March, then Duke of York, the descendant of Lionel duke of Clarence, the second son of Edward III. which occasioned the wars between the houses of York and Lancaster, under the device of the white rose and red. The next year, the dukes of Exeter, Surrey, and Albemarle, the earls of Salisbury and Gloucester, the Bishop of Carlisle, and Sir Thomas Blount, the friends of Richard, formed a conspiracy, in order to assassinate Henry, and restore Richard to the throne: but being discovered, and their whole scene frustrated, they assembled an army of 40,000 men, and set up Maudlin, a priest whose person resembled Richard, to pretend that he was Richard himself; but in this they also failed; most of the leaders being taken and beheaded, and Maudlin being hanged at London. This conspiracy hastened the death of the unfortunate king Richard, who was soon after basely murdered at Pontefract. In 1402, Henry caused Sir Roger Clarendon, the natural son of Edward the Black Prince, and several others, to be put to death for maintaining that Richard was alive. The same year he married Joanna of Navarre, widow of the duke of Brittany.

About this time the Scots invaded England.

land under the earl of Douglas, but were defeated at Halidown-hill, by the earl of Northumberland, and his son Henry Hotspur, with the loss of above 10,000 men; and in this victory several earls, and many other persons of consequence, were made prisoners; but the king ordering Northumberland to deliver up the prisoners into his hands, the earl was so exasperated, that he, with Henry Percy, surnamed Hotspur, his son, and other lords, agreed to crown Edmund Mortimer, earl of March, whom Owen Glendower kept prisoner in Wales. The rebel army was encamped near Shrewsbury, headed by Henry Hotspur, the earl of Worcester, and the Scotch earl of Douglas: and the king marched directly thither with 14,000 choice troops, headed by himself, the prince of Wales, and the earl of Dunbar; and, on the 22d of July, 1403, at a place afterwards called Battlefield, he obtained so complete a victory, that about 10,000 of the rebels were killed, among whom was the brave Hotspur, who fell by the hands of the prince of Wales. In 1405 another conspiracy was raised, headed by the archbishop of York, the earl of Northumberland, Thomas Mowbray, Earl Marshal, and other noblemen who assembled a large body of troops at York, and published a manifesto, declaring the king a traitor, and that they were resolved to place Mortimer, the lawful heir, on the throne. But this rebellion was soon suppressed by the policy of Ralph Nevil, earl of Westmoreland.

Henry died in the Jerusalem Chamber at Westminster, on the 20th of March, 1413, in the 46th year of his age, and the 14th of his reign, and was interred in the cathedral at Canterbury.

He was of a middle stature, well proportioned, and perfect in all the exercises of arms and chivalry; his countenance was severe rather than serene; and his disposition sour, sullen and reserved. He possessed a great share of courage, fortitude, and penetration: was naturally imperious, though he bridled his temper with caution; superstitious, though without the least tincture of virtue and true religion; and meanly parsimonious, though justly censured for want of economy, and ill-judged profusion. He rose to the throne by perfidy and treason; established his authority in the blood of his subjects; and died a penitent for his sins, because he could no longer enjoy the fruits of them.

His actions had very little worthy or eminent in them; one thing, at least, has fixed an indelible stain on his memory, viz. his being the first burner of heretics.

Remarkable Events in this Reign.

1399. Geoffrey Chaucer, the poet, died.

1407. A

1407. A great plague in London, which swept away above 30,000 inhabitants.

1407. The collars of SS first worn in England.

✿✿✿✿✿

HENRY V.

Surnamed of MONMOUTH.

HENRY V. the eldest son of king Henry IV. was born in 1388, and succeeded his father 1413. Though wild and unruly in his youth, he no sooner obtained the crown, than he proved himself a wise and a warlike prince. He chose a council of state, composed of men of distinguished wisdom, and commanded those who had been the companions of his irregularities, either to change their manners, or never to approach his person. He revived the English title to the crown of France, and in 1415 embarked his army, amounting to 15,000 men, and having landed at Havre de Grace, laid siege to Harfleur, which surrendered in five weeks. Soon after, the French king, having assembled an army six times as numerous as that of Henry, challenged him to fight, and Henry consented, though the French army consisted of 150,000 men, and the English were reduced by sickness to 9,000. The French, therefore, made re-
joicings

joicings in their camp, as if the English were already defeated, and even sent to Henry to know what he would give for his ransom; to which he replied, " a few hours would shew whose care it would be to make that provision." The English, though fatigued with their march, sick of a flux, and almost starved for want of food, were inspired by the example of their brave king, and resolved to conquer or die. On the 25th of October, 1415, the king being encamped near Agincourt, drew up his small army into two lines, the first commanded by the Duke of York, and the second by himself; he disposed his few men to such advantage, and behaved with such extraordinary conduct and courage, that he gained a complete victory, after having been several times knocked down, and in the most imminent danger of losing his life. The English killed upwards of 10,000 men, and took more prisoners than they had men in their army. The English lost only the duke of York, the earl of Suffolk, a few knights, and 400 private men. In 1417, the king, to enable himself to carry on the war, pledged his crown for 100,000 marks, and part of his jewels for 10,000 pounds; then landing at Beville, in Normandy, he reduced Caen, and the next year subdued all Normandy. On May 21, 1420, a treaty was concluded at Troye, which was ratified by the states of France.

By this treaty the dauphin was disinherited, and Henry V. married Catherine of France, and was declared regent of that kingdom, till the death of Charles VI. when he was to take possession of that crown. But notwithstanding this treaty, the war was continued by the dauphin, and the next year Henry advanced into France with 30,000 men; but while he was marching towards the river Loire, he was seized with a pleuritic fever, and was carried to Vincennes, where he expired on the 31st of August, 1422, in the 34th year of his age, after a glorious reign of nine years, four months, and eleven days. His body was conveyed to England, and interred in Westminster-abbey.

The queen dowager, some time after, married Owen Tudor, a Welsh Gentleman, by whom she had Edmund, the father of Henry Earl of Richmond, who became king of England under the name of Henry VII.

King Henry V. was tall and slender, with a long neck, engaging aspect, and limbs of the most elegant turn. He excelled all the youth of that age in agility, and the exercise of arms; was hardy, patient, and laborious. His valour was such as no danger could startle, and no difficulty oppose; nor was his policy inferior to his courage. He managed the dissensions among his enemies with such address, as proved him consummate in

the

the arts of the cabinet. He was chaste, temperate, modest and devout, scrupulously just in his administration, and severely exact in the discipline of his army, upon which he knew his glory and success in a great measure depended. In a word, it must be owned, he was without an equal in the arts of war, policy and government. His great qualities, however, were somewhat obscured by his ambition, and his natural propensity to cruelty.

Remarkable Events in this Reign.

1417. Holborn first paved by the royal command.

1418. A plague in Paris, which carried off 40,000 persons in three months.

1420. Vines and sugar-canes first planted in Madeira.

1422. The two courts of England and France held at Paris.

HENRY VI.

HENRY VI. was born at Windsor, December 6, 1421, and succeeded his father, Henry V. 1422, when but nine months old, and reigned in England under the tutelage of his uncle Humphrey duke of Gloucester, and in France under that

of

of his uncle the duke of Bedford. This unhappy prince was unsuccessful both at home and abroad. His misfortunes began in France, by the death of his grandfather, Charles VI. not quite two months after the death of his father, king Henry, which gave great advantage to the dauphin, who was called Charles VII. and being crowned at Poitiers, disputed with Henry the crown of France; yet for some time the English continued to have great success in that kingdom, and gained the famous battles of Crevant, Verneuille, and Rouvroi; and every thing seemed to promise the entire possession of France, when it was prevented by an unforeseen blow. A girl, known by the name of Joan of Arc, or the maid of Orleans, suddenly appeared at the head of the French army, and in 1429, made the English raise the siege of Orleans. From that moment Henry's interest in France declined. However, he was carried to Paris, and crowned there with a double crown, in the cathedral church, on the 17th December 1430. In 1444, a truce of eighteen months was concluded between the two crowns: afer which king Henry married Margaret of Anjou, daughter of Renatus king of Naples. This was the source of many of his misfortunes; for the king being of a mild and easy temper, and the queen a high-spirited woman, she undertook, with her

favour-

favourites, to govern the kingdom. The English were now every-where defeated, and in 1441, we had no places left in France but Calais, and the earldom of Guines. These losses were principally occasioned by the civil wars which broke out in England. Richard duke of York, who descended on the mother's side from Lionel, the second son of Edward III. claimed a better right to the crown than Henry, who was descended from John of Gaunt, duke of Lancaster, the third son of the same Edward. Henry was defeated, and made prisoner, at St. Alban's, by Richard Plantagenet, duke of York, on the 31st of May, 1455, and a second time at the battle of Northampton, on the 19th of July, 1460. The parliament then determined that Henry should keep the Crown, and be succeeded by the duke of York, but queen Margaret afterwards raised an army in the North, and gained the battle of Wakefield, December 30, 1460, in which the duke of York was killed, and her husband delivered. This turned the scale, and sunk the interest of the house of York. However, Edward earl of March, the son of Richard duke of York, revived the quarrel, and gained a bloody battle at Mortimer's Cross, near Ludlow. In short, the earl of March, after several engagements, was proclaimed king, by the name of Edward IV. by means of the earl of

Warwick,

Warwick, called the Setter-up, and Puller-down of kings.

Henry VI. was of a hale constitution, naturally insensible of affliction, and hackneyed in the vicissitudes of fortune. He was totally free from cruelty and revenge; on the contrary, he frequently sustained personal indignities of the grossest nature, without discovering the least mark of resentment. He was chaste, pious, compassionate, and charitable, and so inoffensive, that the bishop, who was his confessor for ten years, declared that, in all that time, he had never committed any sin that required penance or rebuke. In a word, he would have adorned a cloister, though he disgraced a crown; and was rather respectable for those vices he wanted, than for the virtues he possessed. He founded the college of Eton, near Windsor, and King's College, in Cambridge, for the reception of those scholars who had begun their studies at Eton.

Remarkable Events in this Reign.

1431. May 30. Joan of Arc, the Maid of Orleans, burnt for a witch at Roan.

1434. A great frost, which lasted ten weeks, so that the Thames was frozen over below bridge as far as Gravesend.

1437. A great dearth, when wheat was sold for 2s. 6d. the bushel, and bread was made of fern roots and ivy berries.

1453.

1453. The first lord mayor's show at London.

1459. Engraving and etching on copper invented.

❧❧❧❧❧❧

EDWARD IV.

EDWARD IV. earl of March, was the son of Richard duke of York, and disputed the crown with Henry VI. who was of the house of Lancaster. Between these two families a great number of battles were fought, with different success; but at length Edward obtained the crown, March 5, 1461, by gaining a signal victory over Henry VI. whom he forced to flee into Scotland, with Margaret of Anjou, his consort. He afterwards gained another victory over the same unhappy prince, who, after his defeat, came into England in disguise, hoping to conceal himself there, till he should have an opportunity of escaping by sea. But unfortunately being discovered, and seized at Waddington-Hall, in Lancashire, whilst he was at dinner, he was conducted to London with his legs tied under a horse's belly, and then confined in the Tower. The earl of Warwick, who had chiefly contributed to raise Edward to the throne, was employed by that prince to negociate a marriage for him in France. In the mean time Edward

marrying

marrying Elizabeth, the widow of Sir John Grey, with whom the earl was in love, that nobleman was so exasperated, that he raised a rebellion, in which he twice defeated the king's forces, and afterwards took his majesty prisoner, whom he confined in Mid-. dleham castle; from whence he escaped, and joining Lord Hastings in Lancashire, re-turned to London, when another battle ensued, and Warwick being defeated, was obliged to flee into France; but soon after landing at Dartmouth with a few troops, he soon increased them to 60,000 men; upon which Edward also raised a numerous army at Nottingham; but, as his enemies were advancing, the cry of King Henry being raised in his camp, Edward fled, and escaped into Flanders. Warwick then took Henry out of the Tower, and caused him to be acknowledged king of England. But Edward afterwards returning with a small force, was received at London with acclamations of joy; and Henry, after seven months phantom of sovereignty, was again confined in the Tower. Edward then marched against the Earl of Warwick, and routed his army in a great battle near Barnet, where the earl himself was slain with his brother the marquis of Montacute, and 17,000 of his men.

Some time after, queen Margaret having assembled an army, king Edward defeated her,

her, and took her prisoner with her son prince Edward, who was soon after massacred, in the 18th year of his age; his father king Henry was also murdered in the Tower, or, as others say, died with grief, in the 50th year of his age. Queen Margaret, after being four years confined, was ransomed by her father for 50,000 crowns. Edward caused his brother, the duke of Clarence, to be drowned in a butt of sack. Edward, being now at peace, spent his time in indolence and debauchery. His favourite mistress was Jane Shore, wife to a citizen of London. He died at Westminster on April 9, 1483, in the 42d year of his age, and the 23d year of his reign.

Edward IV. was a prince of the most elegant person, and insinuating address; endowed with the utmost fortitude and intrepidity; possessed of uncommon sagacity and penetration; but like all his ancestors, he was brutally cruel and vindictive, perfidious, lewd, perjured, and rapacious, without one liberal thought, and without one sentiment of humanity.

He was interred at Windsor, in the new chapel, the foundation of which he himself had laid.

Remarkable

Remarkable Events in this Reign.

1461. A tradesman executed for saying he would make his son heir to the crown, alluding to the sign of his house.

1463. The importation of woollen cloths, laces, and ribbands, and other articles manufactured in England, strictly forbidden.

1471. Printing first brought into England by one Caxon, a mercer; and the first printing-press set up in Islip's chapel, Westminster abbey, under the patronage of the abbot.

1472. A plague in England, which carried off more than the fifteen years war.

1478. Another great plague in England, which began in September, and ended in November.

⌊⌊⌊⌊⌊

EDWARD V.

EDWARD V. eldest son of Edward IV. was born in 1470, and succeeded his father in 1483, at 12 years of age. He was at Ludlow when his father died, but being sent for to London, he, on the 4th of May, received the oaths of the principal nobility; and his uncle Richard duke of Gloucester was made protector of the king and kingdom He obliged the queen to deliver up to him the duke of York, the king's brother,

and

and sent them both to the Tower, under pretence of their waiting there till every thing was prepared for the coronation. Meanwhile the duke of Gloucester, by the assistance of the duke of Buckingham, Sir John Shaw, lord mayor of London, and Dr. Shaw, his brother, had the two young princes declared illegitimate, and then caused himself to be acknowledged king of England, pretending to accept of the crown with reluctance ; though he had put to death lord Hastings, for no other crime than his being warmly attached to the young king : however, as that nobleman was greatly beloved by the people, Gloucester pretended that his ambition and sorceries endangered the kingdom. The queen and Jane Shore were accused as his colleagues, and the latter was taken into custody, but soon after released, on doing penance. Sir Roger Brackenbury, lieutenant of the Tower, refusing to comply with Richard's cruel designs, he for one night only gave the command of that fortress to Sir James Tyrrell, and he procured two villains, who in the dead of the night entered the chamber where the princes lay, and smothered them in bed. Thus died Edward V. having reigned only two months and twelve days.

RICHARD III.

RICHARD III. king of England, surnamed *Crook-back*, was the brother of
Edward IV. and raised himself to the throne
by a series of the most inhuman murders.
Henry VI. and the young prince his son,
with several noblemen of the first rank, died
while he was duke of Gloucester, to prepare the way for his usurping the throne
from Edward V. He was proclaimed king
on the 20th of June, 1483, in the 32d year
of his age, but delayed the ceremony of his
coronation till the 6th of July, and soon after
caused Edward V. and his brother, whom
he had before declared to be bastards, to
be smothered in the Tower. The same
year, having broke his promise to the duke
of Buckingham, who had been greatly in-
strumental in placing him on the throne,
that nobleman took up arms against him,
in order to assist Henry earl of Richmond,
the last branch of the house of Lancaster, to
obtain the crown; but the duke being betrayed by a fellow who had been his servant,
for the sake of a very great reward offered
for apprehending him, he was beheaded at
Salisbury without any legal process. However, the earl of Richmond, obtaining assistance from the duke of Brittany, sailed
from St. Maloes on the 12th of October,

with

with 5000 men and 40 ships ; but his fleet
being dispersed, he returned to Brittany,
and afterwards to France. Richard, in the
mean time, sacrificed many persons to his
revenge, and sent Sir Ralph Ashton into
the western counties, with power to execute
upon the spot all such persons whom he
even suspected to be guilty of high treason ;
and finding that the earl of Richmond,
founded his projects on the hopes of marrying Elizabeth, daughter of Edward IV.
he resolved to marry that princess himself,
though he was already married to the widow
of Edward prince of Wales, the son of Henry
VI. whom he himself murdered ; and therefore now, in order to obtain Elizabeth, he is
said to have poisoned his queen. The earl
of Richmond, however, landed in Wales,
with 2000 men, which increased to 5000,
and with this small army engaged the king's
forces, which consisted of 13,000 men, at
Bosworth, in Leicestershire : but the earl
being joined by Lord Stanley and his brother with fresh troops, he gained a complete victory : when Richard seeing the day
was lost, rushed into the midst of his enemies, and died with his sword in his hand.
The crown, being found after the battle, was
placed on the head of the earl of Richmond ;
and Richard's body was taken up entirely
naked, and covered with blood and dirt, in
which condition it was thrown across a horse,

 carried

carried to Leicester, and interred without the least ceremony. Thus fell Richard, on the 22d of August, 1485, in the 34th year of his age, after an infamous reign of two years. He was buried in the Grey-friars church at Leicester.

Richard III. was, through the whole course of his life, restrained by no principle of justice or humanity; and it appears that he endeavoured to maintain the crown by the same fraud and violence by which he obtained it.

He certainly possessed an uncommon solidity of judgment, a natural fund of eloquence, the most acute penetration, and such courage as no danger could dismay. He was dark, silent, and reserved; and so much master of dissimulation, that it was almost impossible to dive into his real sentiments when he wanted to conceal his designs. His stature was small; his aspect cloudy, severe, and forbidding; one of his arms was withered, and one shoulder higher than the other, from which circumstance of deformity he acquired the epithet of *Crook-back*. He was the last king of the Plantagenet race, who had swayed the sceptre ever since Henry II.

Remarkable Events in this Reign.

1483. Post-horses and stages first established.

An inundation of the River Severn, which

which lasted ten days: and men, women,
and children were carried away in their beds
by the violence of it,

ᘓᘓᘓᘓᘓ

HENRY VII.

HENRY VII. king of England, was the
son of Edmund Tudor, earl of Richmond, and of Margaret of the house of Lancaster. He was crowned on the 30th of October, 1485. He married Elizabeth, daughter of Edward IV. by which the claims of
the houses of York and Lancaster were united. However, fresh troubles broke out, and
the enemies to Henry attempted twice to
dethrone him, by setting up two pretenders;
the first was one Lambert Simnel, a baker's
son, who assumed the title of earl of Warwick, and pretended to be the son of the duke
of Clarence, brother to Edward IV. but being defeated and taken prisoner, was made
king Henry's turnspit. The other was an
adventurer, named Perkin Warbeck, who per-
sonated Richard duke of York, Edward the
Fifth's brother, who was murdered in the
Tower, and being at length taken prisoner,
was hanged at Tyburn. Henry assisted the
emperor Maximilian against Charles VIII.
of France; he made war on the Scots; instituted the band of gentlemen pensioners; built

G 3   the

the chapel adjoining to Westminster abbey, which still bears his name ; and founded several colleges, by which he obtained the character of a pious prince, and a friend to learning, though he was remarkable for his avarice, and grievously oppressing the people by numberless exactions. He died at Richmond palace, which he had caused to be erected, the 22d of April, 1509, aged 52, in the 24th year of his reign, and was succeeded by his second son Henry VIII. He also left two daughters, Margaret, who was married to James IV. king of Scotland, and Mary, who married the French king Lewis XII.

Henry VII. was tall, straight and well-shaped, though slender ; of a grave aspect, and saturnine complexion. He inherited a natural fund of sagacity, which was improved by study and experience ; nor was he deficient in personal bravery, or political courage. He was cool, close, cunning, dark, distrustful, and designing ; and of all the princes who had sat upon the English throne, the most sordid, selfish, and ignoble. At the same time, it must be owned he was a wise legislator, chaste, temperate, assiduous in the exercise of religious duties ; decent in his deportment, and exact in the administration of justice, when his own private interest was not concerned ; though he frequently used religion and justice as cloaks for perfidy and oppression. His soul was continually actuated

by

by two ruling passions, equally base, and un-
kingly, namely the fear of losing his crown,
and the desire of amassing riches ; and these
motives influenced his whole conduct.

Remarkable Events in this Reign.

1485. Yeomen of the guards first instituted.

A new disease, called the sweating sickness, began in September, and, though
it continued little more than a month, carried off many thousands; particularly in
London.

1487. The court of Star-chamber first instituted.

1488. The Cape of Good Hope discovered.

1489. Maps and sea-charts first brought
into England by Bartholomew Columbus.

1491. Greek first introduced into England.

1492. America discovered by Christopher
Columbus, a Genoese, Oct. 11.

1497. The East Indies discovered by a
Portuguese; and Florida, Jamaica, Porto
Rico, Trinidad, and Newfoundland, by Ca-
bot, a Venetian.

1497. The West Indies discovered by
Columbus.

1500. A great plague in England, which
occasioned the king and court to remove to
Calais,

Calais, and swept off upwards of 30,000 people in London.

1504. Henry the Seventh's chapel, at the east of Westminster-abbey, built.

1505. Shillings first coined in England.

1507. The island of Madagascar discovered by the Portuguese.

The Dutch by treaty excluded from fishing on the coast of England.

A sweating sickness raged.

1509. King Henry, a little before his death, published a general pardon to all his subjects, released all debtors out of prison, who did not owe more than forty shillings to any one man, paying their creditors out of his own purse; and by his will commanded his successor to make restitution to all men whom he had wronged by his extortions, to which his son paid no great regard.

He left behind him 1,800,000 pounds, which he had extorted from his subjects; but to make some amends, he converted the palace of the Savoy into an hospital, and built some religious houses.

HENRY VIII.

H ENRY VIII. king of England, was born June 28, 1491, and succeeded his father Henry VII. on April 22, 1509. His

marriage

marriage with Catharine of Arragon, relict of his brother Arthur, was solemnized the beginning of June, as was the coronation of both king and queen on the 24th of the same month. He joined the Emperor Maximilian against Lewis XII. king of France ; defeated the French at the battle of the Spurs, in 1513, and took Terouenne and Tournay. At his return to England, he marched against the Scots, and defeated them at Flodden, September 9, after an obstinate and bloody battle, in which James IV. of Scotland was slain. In 1514, Henry VIII. concluded a treaty of peace with Lewis XII. and gave his sister Mary in marriage. He wrote a book against Luther, *Of the Seven Sacraments*, &c. It was presented to Pope Leo X. in full consistory, who, for his service done the church, bestowed on Henry and his successors the title of *Defender of the Faith*. This title being afterwards confirmed by parliament, the kings of England have borne it ever since.

A war breaking out between the Emperor, Charles V. and the French king Francis I. Henry at first took the part of the emperor, but afterwards, at the solicitation of cardinal Wolsey, contracted a strict friendship with Francis, and in 1528, laboured to procure the deliverance of Pope Clement VII. By the assistance of Wolsey, he, in 1533, divorced Catherine of Arragon, and married Anne

Anne Boleyn, on which he was excommunicated by the Pope. Henry, enraged at this excommunication, abolished the papal authority in England; refused to pay the see of Rome his annual tribute; ordered the dissolution of monasteries, obliged the clergy to acknowledge him head of the church, and those who refused were either banished or put to death: among these last were, the learned Sir Thomas Moore, lord chancellor of England, and Fisher bishop of Rochester. The reformation thus begun in this kingdom was completed in the reign of Elizabeth. Some time after, being charmed with the beauty of Jane Seymour, he caused Anne Boleyn to be beheaded; but Jane dying in childbed of prince Edward, he married Anne of Cleves, whom he afterwards divorced. He then married Catharine Howard, the duke of Norfolk's daughter, whom he caused to be beheaded, under pretence that he had not found her a virgin; but his real motive was that of having conceived a violent passion for Catharine Parr, a young widow of great beauty. A war breaking out between him and the Scots, who were assisted by the French, Henry, in 1545, took Bologne from the latter, and burnt Leith and Edinburgh. He founded six new bishoprics, viz. Westminster, Oxford, Peterborough, Bristol, Chester and Gloucester; all of which, except Westminster, are still episcopal sees. He

united

united Wales to England, and died January
29, 1547, aged 56, after a reign of 38 years,
and was interred at Windsor with idle pro-
cessions, and childish pageantry, which in
those days passed for real taste and magnificence.

Henry VIII. before he became corpulent,
was a prince of goodly personage, and commanding aspect, rather imperious, than dignified. He excelled in all the exercises of
youth, and possessed a good understanding,
which was not much improved by the nature
of his education. In the first year of his
reign, his pride and vanity seemed to domi-
neer over all his other passions, though from
the beginning he was impetuous, headstrong,
impatient of contradiction and advice. He
was rash, arrogant, prodigal, vain-glorious,
pedantic, and superstitious. He delighted
in pomp and pageantry, the baubles of a weak
mind. His passions, soothed by adulation,
rejected all restraint ; and as he was an utter
stranger to the finer feelings of the soul, he
gratified them at the expence of justice and
humanity, without remorse or compunction.
From the abject compliance of his subjects he
acquired the most despotic authority over
them, and became rapacious, arbitrary, froward, fretful, and so cruel, that he seemed
to delight in their blood.

Remarkable

Remarkable Events in this Reign.

1500. Gardening introduced into England from the Netherlands, from whence vegetables were before imported.

1512. Sir Edward Howard appointed the first lord high admiral.

A royal navy office established.

1516. So great a frost in England, that carts passed over the Thames on the ice.

1517. A sweating sickness raged with such force, that the patients were usually carried off in three hours.

The reformation in religion begun by Martin Luther.

1518. New Spain discovered by Fernandez Cortez.

1521. Muskets first invented.

A dearth in England, when wheat was sold at 20 shillings per quarter.

The Sea overflowed the dikes of Holland, drowned 72 villages, and above 100,000 people.

1523. The College of Physicians in London instituted.

1525. A severe frost, after great winds and rains, when many lost the use of their limbs, and some perished with cold.

Whitehall built by cardinal Wolsey.

1529. The name of Protestants begun.

1530. St. James's Palace built.

Secretary of State's office instituted.

1535. Brass

1535. Brass cannon first cast in England.

1537. The Bible printed in English, and ordered to be set up in churches.

1538. Leaden pipes for the conveyance of water, invented.

1542. A great mortality, and so great a drought, that small rivers were dried up; the Thames was so shallow, that the salt water flowed above London bridge.

1543. Mortars and cannon cast in iron, the first that were ever made in England.

EDWARD VI.

EDWARD VI. king of England, and the only son of Henry VIII. by Jane Seymour, was born October 12, 1537, and ascended the throne at nine years of age, at which time he was well skilled in the Latin, and French tongues, and had obtained some knowledge of the Greek, Italian, and Spanish. His person was very beautiful; he had great sweetness of temper, and was remarkable for his piety and humanity. He was proclaimed January 31, 1547, and crowned February 20. He was committed to the care of sixteen persons, whom Henry had nominated regents of the kingdom, the principal of whom was the earl of Hertford,

H   the

the king's uncle by the mother's side, who was soon after created duke of Somerset. The young queen of Scotland was demanded in marriage for king Edward, but the same proposal being made by France, in behalf of the dauphin, she was sent into that kingdom; on which the duke of Somerset invaded Scotland, and routed the Scots army at Mussleberg. The great power of the duke of Somerset raised him many enemies, the chief of whom was his brother, Thomas lord Seymour; and articles of accusation being exhibited against him, he was attainted in parliament, condemned, and beheaded, without being brought to an open trial. However, the duke of Somerset himself was, some time after, impeached, and charged with a design to seize the king, and to imprison the earl of Warwick: for this he was condemned, and the young king being in a manner forced to sign the sentence, he was executed on the 22nd of January, 1551. The earl of Warwick, now duke of Northumberland, succeeded to the duke of Somerset's power, and at length, on the king's being taken ill of the measles, married lord Guildford Dudley, his fourth son, to the lady Jane Grey, eldest daughter to the duke of Suffolk, and persuaded Edward to settle the crown on her; his sisters, Mary and Elizabeth, having been both declared illegitimate during the life of their father; and the prince,

hoping

hoping to save the reformation from impending destruction, appointed her as his successor, and soon after died of a consumption, July 6, 1553, in the 16th year of his age, having reigned six years, five months, and nine days. He continued firmly attached to those principles of the reformation which he had imbibed while young, and which made a great progress in his reign. He confirmed his father's grant of Christ's and St. Bartholomew's hospitals, and founded Bridewell and St. Thomas's hospitals. He also founded several schools, which were mostly endowed out of the church-lands.

Remarkable Events in this Reign.

1548. A great plague in London.

1549. Anabaptists came into England.

Horse guards instituted.

1551. A sweating sickness raged throughout England.

1551. An earthquake happened in Surry.

1552. Crowns and half-crowns first coined.

1553. This was such a plentiful year, that a barrel of beer, with the cock, were sold for sixpence, and four great loaves for one penny.

Edward kept a journal, which is preserved in the British Museum, in which he regularly entered all the important transactions of his reign.

 MARY.

MARY.

MARY, queen of England, daughter of Henry VIII. and Catharine of Arragon, was born the 18th of February, 1515. On her father's marrying Anne Boleyn, she was declared illegitimate. After the death of Edward VI. in 1553, lady Jane Grey was proclaimed queen of England; but Mary, promising that no change should be made in religion, obtained the crown, and some time after, lady Jane, with the lord Dudley, and other persons of quality, were beheaded. Soon after Mary's accession to the throne, she married Philip II. afterwards king of Spain, son of the emperor Charles V. who was then living; and in violation of the most sacred promises, began a dreadful persecution of the protestants, which was carried on by Bonner, bishop of London, and Gardner, bishop of Winchester. Great numbers of persons suffered martyrdom at the stake, among whom were Cranmer, Ridley, Latimer, Hooper, and Ferrar; and all the prisons in the kingdom were crowded with pious sufferers, who chose to submit to persecution, rather than violate their consciences. Even the princess Elizabeth was closely watched, and obliged to conceal her religious sentiments.

Amidst these dreadful proceedings, Mary
was

was far from being happy; a continual disagreement with her husband, who was
younger than she, and of whom she was
passionately fond, with the loss of Calais,
which was taken by the French, threw her
into a complication of disorders, of which
she died without issue the 17th of November, 1558, in the 43d year of her age, after
a bloody reign of five years, four months,
and eleven days.

In the four years in which the persecution
lasted, near 300 persons were put to death;
viz. one archbishop, four bishops, 21 divines, eight gentlemen, 84 artificers, 100 hus-
bandmen, servants, and labourers, 26 wives,
20 widows, nine virgins, two boys, and two
infants; besides which, several died in prison, and many were whipped or otherwise
cruelly treated.

The characteristics of Mary were bigotry
and revenge; added to this, she was proud,
imperious, froward, avaricious, and wholly
destitute of every agreeable qualification.
She was buried at Westminster, in the chapel of her grandfather, Henry VII.

Remarkable Events in this Reign.

1555. Coaches first used in England.

1558. July. Two little towns near Nottingham beat down by thunder, and hail-
stones fell which measured fifteen inches in
circumference.

ELIZABETH.

ELIZABETH, daughter of Henry VIII. and Anne Boleyn, was born September 8, 1533, and ascended the throne November 17, 1558. This princess was crowned with great solemnity, on the 15th of January, 1559.

As there were many troubles then in foreign states, chiefly on account of religion, she assisted the Protestants in Scotland, France, and the Low Countries, against their respective sovereigns, or the governing parties, by whom they were cruelly oppressed and persecuted. The queen of Scots, and the dauphin her husband, had, by order of Henry II. of France, taken the arms of England, with the titles of sovereigns of that kingdom. This made Elizabeth consider Mary as a dangerous rival, whereupon, in 1560, she entered into a treaty with the Scotch mal-contents, and sent an army into Scotland, to break the measures of her enemies, which had the desired success. Some time after, she assisted the Huguenots in France. By these means Elizabeth kept both France and Scotland so employed, that they could find no opportunity to put their schemes in execution of dethroning her. She always kept a good fleet in readiness against any invasion,

vasion, and effectually secured the love of her subjects, whom she looked upon as her only support. The queen of Scots, being defeated in 1568, by the forces raised by the mal-contents in that kingdom, was obliged to flee into England, where the queen kept her prisoner many years.

In 1569, a rebellion broke out in the North, under the earls of Westmoreland and Northumberland, and Dacres, a Northern gentleman who intended to have set Mary queen of Scots on the throne, and to have restored the popish religion. This rebellion, however, was suppressed, and the earl of Northumberland was beheaded, as was also the duke of Norfolk in 1572, who had been released out of the Tower, and engaged again in a conspiracy against the queen.

The year 1571 passed chiefly in a negociation for a marriage between Elizabeth and the duke of Anjou, second son to Catharine de Medicis, and brother to Charles IX. of France. Both Charles and Elizabeth found their account in this negotiation, though neither of them intended it should take effect. Charles's design was to amuse the Protestants, particularly the Huguenots, with whom he had made a perfidious peace, till he had drawn them into the snare, in order to destroy them by treachery, when he found it difficult to do it by open force. Queen Elizabeth

Elizabeth entered into the negotiation of the match to please her ministers, who were continually pressing her to marry, in order to cut off all hopes from the queen of Scots, and to dishearten her enemies. However, a defensive alliance was concluded between the two crowns. Charles died and was succeeded by the duke of Anjou, by the name of Henry III. with whom queen Elizabeth renewed the league between the two crowns, but secretly supplied the prince of Conde, with money for the Huguenots.

Some time after, another negotiation was carried on for a marriage between her and the duke of Alençon, now duke of Anjou, Henry's brother, even to the signing of her marriage articles, and the duke came over in person; but it was all broke off on a sudden.

In 1577, she assisted the people of the Low Countries, who were grievously oppressed by the duke of Alva, the king of Spain's general, and who was endeavouring to extirpate the protestants; she lent them 100,000l. sterling, to enable them to carry on the war. The next year several companies of volunteers were formed in England, who went over to serve the States, with the queen's approbation. Some years after, she sent a considerable body of forces, under the earl of Leicester, but he not being agreeable to the States, was recalled, and lord Willoughby was appointed general of the English

forces

forces in his room: this war terminated in the total revolt of seven of those provinces from the dominion of Spain, which afterwards made the most considerable republic in the world. The pope excommunicated the queen; and the king of Spain and the duke of Guise formed a league with the Roman pontiff to invade England, dethrone Elizabeth, and set up the queen of Scots in her room. In the mean time, several plots were set on foot by the popish emissaries to take away her life, for which several priests, jesuits, and others, were executed. In 1585, the queen sent Sir Francis Drake to America, who took several places in the Spanish West Indies. In 1586, she made an alliance with the king of Scotland, for their mutual defence, and the security of the protestant religion. This year died the learned and ingenious Sir Philip Sidney, of a wound he received in a battle in the Low Countries.

Babington's conspiracy, in which were engaged several popish priests from the seminaries abroad, was discovered; and they were, to the number of fourteen, arraigned, condemned, and executed. It was laid for an invasion, to kill Elizabeth, free the queen of Scotland, and set her on the throne. As the queen of Scots appeared, by letters and otherwise, to have been concerned in this conspiracy, it was resolved now to prosecute her on an act of parliament made the preceding

ceding year, whereby the person for whom, or by whom, any thing should be attempted against the queen, was liable to death. Commissioners were accordingly sent to try her at Fotheringay-castle, in Northamptonshire, (where she was then in custody) who passed sentence upon her, on October 25. Four days after, it was approved and confirmed by parliament; on December 6, it was proclaimed through the whole kingdom; and on February 8th following, the sentence was executed upon her in the hall of the castle, by severing her head from her body, which she suffered with equal calmness and resolution.

In 1588, the king of Spain, encouraged by pope Sextus V. sent a great fleet, to which they had given the title of the invincible armada, to invade England. It consisted of 130 great ships, 20 caravels, and 10 salves, having above 20,000 soldiers on board, with seamen, ammunition, and provision in proportion. To oppose this armament 20,000 men were dispersed along the southern coasts, and an army of 22,000 foot, and 1000 horse were encamped at Tilbury, were the queen reviewed them, and made a very engaging speech to them. Another army of 34,000 foot, and 2000 horse, was appointed to guard the queen's person, and a considerable fleet was fitted out under the command of lord Howard as admiral, and Drake, Hawkins, and Forbisher, vice-admirals;

admirals; while Seymour was sent with forty English and Dutch ships, to the coast of Flanders, to hinder the Prince of Parma from joining the Spanish fleet.

On the 19th of July, the Spanish fleet, commanded by the duke of Medina Sidonia, entered the channel, when the English fleet kept close to them, and soon took some of their ships. On July 24th there was a brisk engagement. On the 27th the Spanish fleet came to an anchor off Calais, expecting in vain the prince of Parma to put to sea with his army, and make a descent on England, as it had been agreed. The English fleet, now consisting of 140 ships, followed them; and the English admiral, in the night, sent eight fire-ships among them, which so terrified them, that they cut their cables, and put to sea in the utmost confusion; the English admiral took the Galeass, and the commander of it was slain. In short the whole fleet was dispersed, and the Spaniards resolved to make the best of their way home. Of this prodigious armament, only fifty-three ships returned to Spain, and those in a shattered condition. Queen Elizabeth went in state to St. Paul's, to return thanks to God for this decisive victory.

In 1594, Roderic Lopez, a Jew, who was the queen's physician, two Portuguese, and Patrick Cullen, an Irishman, were bribed by the Spanish governors of the Netherlands, to take her off by poison ; but the plot being discovered, the conspirators were seized and executed ; as were Edmund York and Richard Williams, the next year, for undertaking to commit a similar crime on the promise of 40,000 crowns from the Spanish governors.

In 1596, the queen sent a fleet and army under Howard, the earl of Essex, and Sir Walter Raleigh, to the coasts of Spain, which plundered Cadiz, burnt the merchant ships at Port Real, took and destroyed thirteen Spanish men of War, and did other considerable damage. In 1598, Henry IV. of France, having made a separate peace with the king of Spain, queen Elizabeth and the States entered into a new treaty to carry on the war against that monarch by themselves. On the 25th of February, 1601, Robert Devereux, earl of Essex, was beheaded.

Queen Elizabeth died on March 24, 1603, in the 70th year of her age, and the 45th of her reign, after having named the Scottish monarch for her successor. She was interred with great magnificence in the chapel of Henry VII. at Westminster.

The papists represent Elizabeth as a monster of cruelty, avarice, and lasciviousness ; which is not to be wondered at, considering her severity to them. It is, indeed, difficult to excuse her beheading Mary queen of Scots, and the severity she sometimes made use of

both

both against the papists and the protestant dissenters: but she certainly understood the art of governing in an eminent degree; and her reign was the school of able ministers, great statesmen, and distinguished warriors. She understood the Greek, Latin, French, Spanish, and Dutch languages, and possessed a deep, penetrating, and elevated mind. Her conversation was sprightly and agreeable, her judgment solid, her apprehension acute, her application indefatigable, and her courage invincible. Yet her glorious reign, on which Providence for a long time poured innumerable blessings, ended in a most dismal melancholy, which some are of opinion, was occasioned by the death of the earl of Essex. This queen makes a considerable figure among the learned ladies. Besides a variety of other things, she wrote a Comment on Plato, and translated into Latin two of the Orations of Isocrates, and a play of Euripides.

Remarkable Events of this Reign.

1560. June 15. The spire of St. Paul's, in London, destroyed by lightning.

1563. Knives first made in England.

1565. July 16. A violent storm of thunder and hail happened, which destroyed 500 acres of corn in Chelmsford.

1566. June 7. The foundation of the
Royal

Royal Exchange, in London, laid by Sir Thomas Gresham.

1568. A new translation of the Bible published.

1571. Feb. 17. A great earthquake in Herefordshire, when Marclay-hill was removed from the place where it stood, and continued in motion two days; it carried along the trees, hedges, sheep, &c. and overturned Kyneton chapel.

1574. A great dearth in England.

1583. Jan. 23. An earthquake in Dorsetshire, which removed a considerable piece of ground.

1588. The art of making paper introduced into England.

1590. Telescopes, and the art of weaving stockings invented.

1592. The Thames was almost dry.

1593. Twenty-eight thousand people died of the plague in London.

1596. An earthquake in Kent.

1597. Watches first brought into England from Germany.

A great plague in London and its suburbs, which swept off 17,890 persons.

JAMES I.

JAMES VI. of Scotland, and First of England, son of Henry Stuart and Mary queen of Scotland, was born June 19, 1566, and ascended the English throne in 1603, after the death of queen Elizabeth, who had nominated him for her successor, as being her nearest relation; for he was descended from the eldest son of king Henry VII. He united Scotland to England, and took the title of king of Great Britain. In 1604, he ordered all popish priests to leave England on pain of death.

In 1605, a plot was discovered of a design to blow up the parliament house, 36 barrels of gunpowder being put in a cellar under the lords' house, which had been hired for that purpose, and covered over with coals, billets, and faggots. Guy Faux, who was to have set fire to the train, was discovered in a cloak and boots, with a dark lanthorn, tinderbox, and matches in his pocket. Himself and his accomplices were executed in January following; as were also Oldcorn, and Garnet, two jesuits, for concealing and abetting the plot.

In 1606, king James caused the oath of allegiance to be drawn up; and, in 1621, summoned a parliament, in which were formed the two parties called Whigs and

Tories.

Tories. He suffered the Dutch to take Amboyna, and to massacre the English inhabitants without shewing any resentment, and caused the brave Sir Walter Raleigh to be put to death for his successful expeditions against the Spaniards. He was educated by the famous Buchanan, and prided himself on his skill in Latin and school divinity: though the works he published prove that he was but an indifferent writer. These works principally consist of several tracts, which are printed in one volume in folio, and contain an attempt to prove that monarchs have a right to be absolute, and independent of their subjects; on the heinous sin of taking tobacco; on witchcraft, &c. Mr. Walpole observes, that " There is not the least suspicion that the folio, under the name of James I. is not of his own composition; for though Roger Ascham," says he, " may have corrected or assisted periods of his illustrious pupil, no body can imagine that Buchanan dictated a word of the Demonologia, or of the polite treatise entitled, " A Counterblast to Tobacco." Quotations, puns, witticisms, superstition, oaths, vanity, prerogative, and pedantry, the ingredients of all his sacred majesty's performances, were the pure produce of his own capacity, and deserving all the incense offered to such immense erudition by the divines of his age, and the flatterers of his court." He died

at

at Theobald's, March 27, 1625, aged 55, after having reigned 22 years in England, and was succeeded by his son Charles I.

James I. was of a middle stature inclining to corpulency; his forehead was high, his beard scanty, his aspect mean, his address awkward, and his appearance slovenly. There was nothing dignified either in the composition of his mind or person. In the course of his reign he exhibited repeated instances of his ridiculous vanity, prejudices, profusion, folly, and littleness of soul. All that we can add in his favour is, that he was averse to cruelty and injustice; very little addicted to excess, temperate in his meals, kind to his servants, and even desirous of acquiring the love of his subjects, by granting that as a favour which they claimed as a privilege. His reign, though ignoble to himself, was happy to his people, who were enriched by commerce which no war interrupted.

Remarkable Events in this Reign.

1603. 35,244 persons died of the plague in London.

The office of master of the ceremonies instituted.

1604, and 1605. The plague destroyed 68,596 persons in London.

1609. A frost happened, which lasted

four months; the Thames was so frozen that heavy carriages passed over it.

1611. Baronets first created in England.

The present translation of the Bible finished.

1619. The circulation of the blood confirmed by Dr. Harvey.

1620. Copper money first used in England.

1621. The broad silk manufacture from raw silk, introduced into England.

In the 14th year of this reign, Sir Hugh Middleton, a private citizen of London, supplied part of the city with excellent water conveyed in an aqueduct from Ware in Hertfordshire, now known by the name of the New River.

CHARLES I.

CHARLES I. king of Great Britain, was born at Dumferling, in Scotland, November 19, 1600. He succeeded his father, James I. in 1625, and the same year married Henrietta of France, the daughter of Henry V. Two years after, he sent assistance to the French calvinists to prevent the taking of Rochelle; but on the reduction of that place a treaty of peace was concluded between the two crowns. There was nothing

thing but continual struggles between the king, who wanted to assume to himself the absolute power of disposing of his subjects' property, and leaving their grievances unredressed, and the parliament who were willing to grant the necessary supplies, provided their grievances were redressed, and the right privileges of the subject secured, which at last produced a civil war. Aug. 22, 1642, the king, in a solemn manner, set up his standard at Nottingham. On June 1, 1645, was fought the famous battle of Naseby, which decided the quarrel between the king and the parliament, wherein the forces of the latter gained a complete victory. Upon the approach of Lord Fairfax, to lay siege to Oxford, his majesty threw himself into the hands of the Scots army. Oxford surrendered June 22, 1646, and the few remaining garrisons soon after. The parliament then consulted how to get the king out of the hands of the Scots, and to send them back into their own country. After several debates about the disposal of his person, the Scots having received 200,000l. August 8, 1646, delivered him up to the commissioners of the parliament of England, who were sent down to Newcastle to receive him. The same day their army began to march for Scotland, and the king was conveyed to Holmby-house, in Northamptonshire. He

was

was afterwards removed to Hampton-court, whence he made his escape and fled to the Isle of Wight. He had not been there long when a party of Cromwell's soldiers seized him and conveyed him first to Hurst castle, then to Windsor, and at last to St. James's palace. The next day he was brought to his trial, and sentence of death was passed upon him; pursuant to which he was beheaded before the banqueting house, at Whitehall, on the 30th of January, 1643, in the 49th year of his age, and the 24th of his reign. His body was carried to Windsor, and privately interred in St. George's chapel. Such was the unfortunate end of Charles I. king of England. He was a prince of a middling stature, robust and well proportioned. His hair was of a dark colour, his forehead high, his complexion pale, his visage long, and his aspect melancholy. His perception was clear and acute, his judgment solid and decisive. In his private morals he was altogether unblemished and exemplary. He was merciful, modest, chaste, temperate, religious, and personally brave; and we may join the noble historian in saying, " He was the worthiest gentleman, the best master, the best friend, the best husband, the best father, and the best christian of the age in which he lived." He suffered himself to be guided by counsellors who were not only inferior to himself in knowledge and judgement,

ment, but generally proud, partial, and inflexible ; and he paid too much deference to the advice and desires of his consort, who was superstitiously attached to the errors of popery.

Remarkable Events in this Reign.

1625. A great plague in London, which swept away 35,417 persons.

1630. May 29. A bright star appeared, and shone all the day.

1625. Thomas Parr was presented to the king, being 152 years of age, and in perfect health. He died at London, November 15. He had lived in ten reigns.

1636. A plague in London.

1643. Excise on beer, ale, &c. first imposed by parliament.

THE COMMONWEALTH.

OLIVER CROMWELL was the son of a private gentleman of Huntingdon, and was born the 24th of April, 1599. Being the son of a second brother, he inherited a very small paternal fortune. From accident or intrigue he was chosen member for Cambridge in the long parliament : but he seemed at first to possess no talents for oratory, his person being ungraceful, his

dress

dress slovenly, and his elocution homely, tedious, obscure, and embarrassed. He made up, however, by zeal and perseverance, what he wanted in natural powers; and being endowed with unshaken intrepidity, and much dissimulation, he rose, through the gradations of preferment, to the post of lieutenant-general under Fairfax; but, in reality, possessing the supreme command of the whole army. After several victories, he gained the battle of Naseby; and this, with other successes, soon put an end to the war.

In 1649, Cromwell was sent general into Ireland, and in about nine months, he subdued almost that whole kingdom, and left his son-in-law, Ireton, to complete the conquest. On June 26, 1650, he was appointed general and commander in chief of all the forces of the commonwealth, and set out on his march against the Scots, who had espoused the royal cause, and placed young Charles, the son of their late monarch, on the throne. On Sept. 3, 1651, he totally defeated the royalists at Worcester, when the king himself was obliged to fly. After having undergone an amazing variety of dangers and distresses, he landed safely at Fescamp, in Normandy, no less than forty persons having at different times been privy to his escape. In the mean time, Cromwell, crowned with success, returned to London, where he was

met

met by the speaker of the house, accompanied by the mayor and magistrates of London, in their formalities. He began now to complain of the long parliament, which on the 20th of April, 1653, he dissolved by force; and two days after published a declaration of his reasons, signed by himself and his council of officers. On December 16, he was invested with the title of Lord Protector of the Commonwealth of England, Scotland, and Ireland. He now applied himself to the management of the several parties, and supplied the benches of the courts of Westminster with the ablest lawyers, but acted in the most arbitrary and oppressive manner, where his own interest was concerned. He gave the command of all the forces in Scotland to general Monk, and sent his own son Henry to govern Ireland. In 1655, he sent a powerful fleet, under the command of admiral Penn, and 5000 land forces, commanded by general Venables, to attack the island of Hispaniola. Failing, however, in this, and being driven off the place by the Spaniards, they steered to Jamaica, which was surrendered to them without a blow. In the mean time, admiral Blake performed great actions in the Mediterranean; so that the Protector's reputation was very high abroad.

In 1657, the parliament agreed to offer Cromwell the title of king; but as he found
this

this proposition disagreeable to his best friends, he declined it, and resolved upon a new inauguration, which was accordingly performed in Westminster-hall, June 26, with all the splendor of a coronation. The next year, Dunkirk surrendered to the French, and was delivered into the hands of the English.

His favourite daughter, Mrs. Claypole, died on August 6, 1658, of a languishing disorder, during which she is said to have awakened the horrors of his guilty conscience. He was from that time wholly altered, grew daily more reserved, and suspicious; not indeed without reason; for he found a general discontent prevail through the nation. He wore armour under his clothes, and always kept a pistol in his pocket. He always travelled with hurry, and attended by a numerous guard. He never returned from any place by the road he went, and seldom slept above three nights together in the same chamber. A tertian ague kindly came at last to deliver him from this life of horror and anxiety. He died on the 3d of September, the anniversary of the victories he had obtained at Dunbar, and Worcester; and his death was rendered remarkable by one of the most violent tempests which had blown in the memory of man. He was then fifty-nine years old, and had usurped the government nine years.

Richard

Richard, his son, was the next day proclaimed Lord Protector; but as he wanted resolution to defend that title, he soon signed his abdication in form, and retired to live at first on the continent, and afterwards on his paternal fortune at Cheshunt, in Hertfordshire, where he died in the year 1712.

CHARLES II.

CHARLES II. was born on the 29th of May, 1630. After an exile of twelve years, in France and Holland, he was restored by general Monk, who had rendered himself absolute master of the parliament. On May 29, 1660, he made his triumphal entry into London, and was crowned the following year. In 1692, the marriage between the King and Catharina infanta of Portugal was solemnized. In 1665, war was declared against the Dutch, and on the 3d of June a great victory was obtained over them at sea. The next year, the French king declared war against England. The English fleet, under the command of prince Rupert and the duke of Albemarle, put to sea about the middle of May; and there soon was a most bloody fight with admiral Ruyter, in which the English were worsted. There was another furious engagement in

July,

July, when the English gained a complete victory, destroying above twenty Dutch men of war, and driving the rest into their harbours. In this action the Dutch lost four of their admirals, besides 4000 other officers and seamen; and the loss on the side of the English is said to have been inconsiderable. In August, Sir Robert Holmes burnt two men of war, and 150 sail of merchant ships, belonging to the Dutch.

On September 3, a terrible fire broke out in London, which continuing three days, destroyed 600 streets, including 89 churches, many hospitals and public edifices, and 13,202 dwelling houses. The ruins, comprehending 436 acres of ground, extended from the Tower, along the river, to the Temple church; and north easterly, along the city walls, as far as Holborn-bridge.

On June 11, 1667, the Dutch sailed up the river Medway, as far as Chatham, made themselves masters of Sheerness, and burnt several men of war, together with a magazine full of stores. But king Charles, notwithstanding this piece of treachery, concluded a treaty at Breda, by which the colony of New York, in North America, was ceded by the Dutch to the English. This peace was, however, of a short continuance; for, in the year 1672, king Charles joined with the French, who attacked the Dutch by land, while the English engaged their fleets

at

at sea; but peace was concluded two years after. The year 1684 was almost wholly taken up with prosecutions of persons for speaking ill of the king, the duke of York, and the government; some were fined in large sums, and others pillored. In 1685, the king was seized with an apoplectic fit; and though he was recovered by bleeding, yet he languished only for a few days, and expired on the 6th of February, in the 55th year of his age, after a reign of near twenty-five years. He was buried in Henry the Seventh's chapel, in Westminster abbey. He had no children by his queen, but several by his mistresses.

Charles II. was in his person tall and swarthy, and his countenance marked with strong harsh lineaments. His penetration was keen, his judgment clear, his understanding extensive, his conversation lively and entertaining, and he possessed the talent of wit and ridicule. He was easy of access, polite and affable. Had he been limited to a private station, he would have passed for the most agreeable and best-natured man of the age in which he lived. His greatest enemies allow him to have been a civil husband, an obliging lover, an affectionate father, and an indulgent master; even as a prince, he manifested an aversion to cruelty and injustice. Yet these good qualities were more than overbalanced by

his

weakness and defects. He was a scoffer at religion, and a libertine in his morals; careless, indolent, profuse, abandoned to effeminate pleasure, incapable of any noble enterprize, a stranger to manly friendship and gratitude, deaf to the voice of honour, blind to the allurements of glory, and, in a word, wholly destitute of every active virtue.

Trade and manufactures flourished more in this reign than at any other era of the English monarchy. Industry was also crowned with success, and the people in general lived in ease and affluence.

Remarkable Events in this Reign.

1660. The Royal Society erected and established.

1662. Feb. 18. A great storm in London.

1665. A most terrible pestilence broke out in London, which swept off 68,596 persons.

1666. Tea first used in England.

1667. The king laid the first stone of the Royal Exchange.

1670. This year died Henry Jenkins, of Yorkshire, aged 170.

1671. May 9. Blood attempted to steal the crown out of the Tower, but was apprehended.

1680. A great comet appeared, and from its nearness to the earth, alarmed the inhabitants.

bitants. It continued visible from Nov. 3 to March 9.

1683. A frost which continued thirteen weeks.

◦◦◦◦◦◦◦

JAMES II.

JAMES II. the second son of Charles I. king of Great Britain, and Henrietta the daughter of Henry IV. king of France, was born at London, the 14th of October, 1633, and had the title of duke of York. After the taking of Oxford, in 1646, the parliament committed him to the care of the earl of Northumberland; but he made his escape, dressed like a girl; and flying into Holland, sought protection from his sister the princess of Orange. He afterwards went into France, served under the viscount de Turenne, and gave proofs of a courage worthy of his birth. He also distinguished himself, in 1665, in the Spanish army under Don Juan of Austria. In 1660 he returned to England with his eldest brother king Charles II. was made lord high admiral of the kingdom, and beat the Dutch fleets in 1665, and in 1672: but as he openly professed his adherence to the popish religion, and prevailed upon his brother to take several arbitrary and unpopular measures, the parliament attempted to ex-

K 3   clude

clude him from the succession : but Charles II.
dying on the 6th of February, 1685, the
duke of York was proclaimed king the same
day, under the title of James II. and a
short time after in Scotland, under that of
James VII.   On his accession, he made a
speech to the privy council, promising to
preserve the government both of the church
and state, yet two days after he went publicly to mass.

On the 11th of June, the duke of Mon-
mouth, natural son of king Charles II. landed at Lyme, in Dorsetshire, with only
eighty-three followers, and immediately published a declaration, that his sole motive for
taking arms, was, to preserve the protestant
religion, and to deliver the nation from the
usurpation and tyranny of James duke of
York; and that his mother was actually married to king Charles II.   He thus raised an
army in the west of England; but, being
defeated and taken prisoner, was beheaded
on Tower-hill, July 15, 1695, aged 35 years ;
and those who had espoused his cause were
butchered by military execution under general Kirk, or barbarously executed, by form
of law, under judge Jeffries, who caused
about 600 persons to be hanged ; and the
steeples, town-gates, and roads, were stuck
with the heads and limbs of the sufferers.

James II. shewed great zeal for the restoration of the popish religion in England, and
in

in 1687 published a proclamation, granting liberty of conscience, by which he gave great pleasure to the dissenters, who had been severely persecuted in the preceding reigns; but on its being discovered that this was an artifice intended to favor the popish party, who were soon put into places of honour and profit, they joined with those of the established church in opposing it. The popish priests now appearing publicly in their habits in the streets, and a nuncio arriving from Rome, the whole nation were alarmed, and applied to William Henry of Nassau, prince of Orange, who had married Mary, king James's eldest daughter, and was himself the son of that king's eldest sister. This prince arrived in England, in 1688, when the dissatisfaction against the king was so great, that a considerable part of his army forsook him; and without venturing an engagement, king James privately retired to France; on which the prince of Orange was crowned king of England by the name of William III. Thus was formed the famous period in English history called the Revolution.

In 1689, James II. landed with an army in Ireland in order to render himself master of that kingdom; but having lost the battle of the Boyne, in which king William commanded in person, he was obliged to return to St. Germain's, where he died, Sept. 16, 1701,

1701, aged 68. He was buried in the church of the monastery of the Benedictines, in Paris. James II. wrote memoirs of his own life and campaigns, to the Restoration ; and Memoirs of the English affairs, chiefly naval from the year 1660 to 1673.

James II. was a prince in whom some good qualities were rendered ineffectual, by mistaken notions of the prerogative, excessive bigotry to the religion of Rome, and an inflexible severity of temper. He was brave, steady, resolute, diligent, upright, and sincere, except when warped by religious considerations ; yet, even where religion was not concerned, he appears to have been proud, haughty, vindictive, cruel and unrelenting ; and though he approved himself an obedient and dutiful subject, he certainly became one of the most intolerable sovereigns that ever reigned over a free people.

WILLIAM III.

WILLIAM III. of Nassau, prince of Orange, stadtholder of the United Provinces, king of England, &c. was the son of William of Nassau, prince of Orange, by Mary, the eldest daughter of Charles I. king of England, and was born at the Hague, the 14th of November, 1650. He was
about

about 22 years of age when he was elected stadtholder, and declared general of the Dutch troops, in order to put a stop to the rapidity of the conquests made by Lewis XIV. In 1673, he took the strong town of Naerden, and obliged the French to quit Utrecht, and several considerable places where they had garrisons. He soon afterwards engaged the French at Senef, where he gained great honour by his courage and conduct, and obtained a victory, after a most obstinate engagement. On the 17th of October, 1677, he embarked for England, and on the 4th of November he was married to the princess Mary, eldest daughter of the duke of York. On the 29th of the same month he departed from London, with his princess, and landed at Terbeyde. In August 1678, he attacked and defeated the duke of Luxemburgh, in his quarters, near the abbey of St. Dennis; in the heat of the action he advanced so far, that he was in great danger of being killed. On June 29, 1684, a treaty was signed at the Hague, which put an end to the war.

James duke of York having ascended the throne of England, after the death of his brother Charles II. endeavouring to restore the popish religion, and to destroy the civil and religious liberty of the people, they naturally cast their eyes on the prince of Orange, and applied to him for deliverance; on on which he landed at Torbay, November 5, 1688, and was joyfully received by almost the whole nation.

James now made his escape to France, and after his departure, the lords and commons agreed, after much dispute, that he had abdicated the throne, upon which the prince of Orange, and the princess Mary, were proclaimed king and queen the 13th of Feb. 1689, and crowned the 11th of April following. An attempt was then made by the opposite party to secure Scotland for James II. but on the 26th of May, 1689, the two armies meeting at Killycrankie, in the shire of Perth, lieutenant general Mackay, who commanded for king William, obtained a complete victory; after which the whole island of Great Britain submitted to him. In the mean time, Tyrconnel had disarmed great part of the protestants of Ireland, and formed an army of papists, amounting to 30,000 foot and 8000 horse, while the protestants in the North took up arms, and seizing on Kilmore, Coleraine, Inniskilling, and Londonderry, declared for king William and queen Mary. Things were in this situation, when James landed at Kinsale, March 12, 1688, and made his public entry into Dublin. He soon after put himself at the head of 20,000 men and was twice reinforced by the French, who each time joined him with 5000 men. He took Coleraine

raine and Kilmore, and laid siege to Londonderry ; but soon after returned to meet
his parliament in Dublin, where he passed
an act to attaint 2 or 3000 protestant lords,
ladies, clergymen, and gentlemen of high
treason.   In the mean time, the siege of
Londonderry was vigorously carried on.
The garrison of Inniskilling, at the same
time performed wonders ; particularly the
day before the siege of Derry was raised they
advanced nearly twenty miles to meet about
6000 Irish, and defeated them, killing near
3000, though they themselves were not above
2000, and had not above 20 killed and 50
wounded.   In August, the duke of Schomberg arrived in Ireland with 10,000 men,
took Carrickfergus in four days, and performed several other gallant actions.   In
June 1600 William landed in Ireland with
a gallant army, and on July 1, fought the
memorable battle of the Boyne, in which
though he had the misfortune to lose the brave
duke of Schomberg, he gained a complete
victory over the French and Irish, and
obliged James to retire first to Dublin, and
afterwards to France.   The next year, the
English, under the brave general Gincle,
and other valiant commanders, made themselves masters of Baltimore, passed the Shan-
non amidst the fire of the enemy, and took
Athlone ; and, on July 12, fought the glorious battle of Ahgrim, wherein 4000 Irish,

and

and their general St. Ruth, were slain, and all their tents, arms, &c. were taken. After this entire defeat, Galway surrendered, and Limerick capitulated, by which an end was put to the Irish war, and all Ireland was reduced to the obedience of king William and queen Mary. In the mean time, the French king was pushing his conquests in the Netherlands, and other parts, which made it necessary for king William to go over to the famous congress at the Hague, in the beginning of the year 1691, in order to animate the confederate princes and states. The French were so far before hand with the allies, that they took the strong city of Mons this year, and Namur in the year following; after which was fought the famous battle of Steenkirk, wherein though the French remained masters of the field of battle, yet king William so bravely disputed the victory, that they had scarce any thing else to boast of, the loss being nearly equal on both sides. The king was no sooner gone abroad in 1691, than the Jacobites resumed their favorite scheme, in concert with France, for restoring the late king. But the vigilance of queen Mary and the government, again disconcerted their measures. In July, 1693, was fought the famous battle of Landen, between the allied army, commanded by king William, and the French, under the duke of Luxemburgh: and though the latter were very much superior in number, the former fought with such obstinate bravery, under their prudent and valiant leader, that for some time, they manifestly had the advantage; and it was only the superiority of numbers that at last wrested the victory out of their hands; after this action, the French made themselves masters of Charleroy. On December 28, 1694, queen Mary died of the small-pox, in the 33d year of her age, having reigned near six years jointly with her royal consort. On March 5, she was solemnly interred in the chapel of Henry VII. The year 1695 was glorious to king William and the allies, by the reduction of Namur; marshal Boufflers having thrown himself into it, with a strong reinforcement, the garrison then consisted of 15,000 men, and they were furnished with provisions for several months. Yet king William, having laid siege to it in the beginning of July, carried it on with such vigor, and good conduct, even in the sight of a numerous French army under marshal Villeroy, who had advanced to relieve it, that the town surrendered on August 6, N. S. and the castle in less than a month after. The English fleet under Lord Berkley spread terror this summer along the coasts of France, bombarded St. Maloes, and some other towns; and, in return, Villeroy, by the French king's order, bombarded Brussels. On the 12th of January

L

nuary a double plot was discovered to assassinate the king, and invade the kingdom. Many of the late king's emissaries came over from France, and held consultations with papists and jacobites here, how to murder William : and after several debates on the time, place, and manner of putting their horrid design in execution, they at last agreed to assassinate his majesty in his coach, on some day in February, 1695, in a lane between Brentford and Turnham-green, as he returned from hunting. But happily the whole plot was discovered on the very night before it was to have been executed. At the same time, there was to be an invasion from France ; for which purpose king James was to come to Calais, and the troops, artillery, and stores, were immediately ordered to be embarked ; but, by the news of the assassination-plot having miscarried, and the speedily sending a formidable fleet under admiral Russel, this other part of the design was frustrated, and Calais was soon after bombarded by the English. A treaty of peace was at last happily concluded, and signed at Ryswick by the English, Spanish, French, and Dutch plenipotentiaries, on September 20, 1697, and by the ministers of the emperor, who stood out for some time, on October 20, with as much advantage to the allies as could reasonably be expected. On the 29th of

July,

July, 1700, the young duke of Gloucester, the only remaining child of seventeen, whom the princess Anne had borne, died of a malignant fever, in the 11th year of his age. The king of Spain dying towards the end of this year, the duke of Anjou was declared king of Spain, by the French king, his grandfather. The French, at the same time, overrunning the Spanish Netherlands, both king William and the States were obliged to acknowledge the duke of Anjou's title, in order to gain time. On February 21, 1701, the king, who had been declining in his health for some time, fell from his horse as he was hunting, and dislocated his right collar bone; which, joined with his former indisposition, held him in a languishing state till the 8th of March, when he expired, in the 52d year of his age, after having reigned thirteen years, three weeks, and two days. On the 12th of April following he was interred in Henry the Seventh's chapel, near the remains of his queen. He left no issue.

William III. was of a middle stature, a thin body, and delicate constitution, subject to an asthma and continual cough from his infancy. He had an aquiline nose, sparkling eyes, a large forehead, and a grave, solemn aspect. He was very sparing of speech; his conversation was dry, and his manner disgusting, except in battle, when his deportment was free, spirited, and ani-

mating.

mating.　In courage, fortitude, and equa-
nimity, he rivalled the most eminent warriors of antiquity ; and his natural sagacity
made amends for the defects of his education, which had not been properly superin-
tended.　He was religious, temperate, generally just and sincere, a stranger to violent
transports of passion, and might have passed
for one of the best princes of the age in
which he lived, had he never ascended the
throne of Great Britain.　But the distinguishing criterion of his character was ambition :
to this he sacrificed the punctilios of honour
and decorum, in deposing his father-in-law
and uncle ; and this he gratified at the expence of the nation that raised him to sovereign authority.　He aspired to the honour
of acting as umpire in all the contests of
Europe : and the second object of his attention was the prosperity of that country to
which he owed his birth and extraction.
To sum up his character in a few words ;
William was a fatalist in religion, indefatigable in war, enterprising in politics, dead
to all the generous emotions of the human
heart, a cold relation, an indifferent husband,
a disagreeable man, an ungracious prince,
and an imperious sovereign.

Remarkable Events in this Reign.

1693. Bayonets first used by the French.
1693.

1693. The bank of England established, and the first public lottery drawn.

1694. Stamp duties instituted.

1701. Prussia erected into a kingdom.

ANNE.

THIS amiable and illustrious princess was descended from a race of kings the most ancient of any in Europe. She was the second daughter of James duke of York, afterwards king James II. by Mrs. Anne Hyde, eldest daughter of Edward earl of Clarendon. The duke was privately married to this lady, during his first exile, in 1659. In 1660, she was, by an order of council, declared duchess of York, and to have the precedency of the princess of Orange, and the queen of Bohemia. The duchess died at the palace of St. James's, March 31, 1671 : she had issue by the duke four sons and four daughters; Charles, born October 22, 1660; Mary, born April 30, 1662 ; James, born July 12, 1663; Anne, born February 6, 1664 ; Charles, born July 4, 1665 : Edgar, born September 14, 1667; Henrietta, born January 13, 1669 ; and Catharine, born February 9, 1670 ; of whom Charles, James, Charles, and Henrietta, died in her lifetime, and Edgar and Catharine did not survive her a year; but Mary and Anne

lived

live to be queens of England. The princess Mary was about nine years old, and Anne about seven, at the death of their mother.

On the death of William III. which happened on Sunday, March 8, 1702, the princess Anne was proclaimed queen of Great Britain, France and Ireland, in the cities of London and Westminster, and was crowned on the 23d of April following. During her reign, the honour of the British arms was carried to an amazing height, particularly by the Duke of Marlborough, who humbled the pride of France, by a number of the most glorious victories. The nation being at the same time at war with Spain, the duke of Ormond and Sir George Rooke took Vigo, when eleven French men of war were burnt, and ten taken: six galleons were sunk and eleven taken. On the 24th of July, 1704, Sir George Rooke took Gibraltar, after a siege of two days. The next year the earl of Peterborough took the city of Barcelona, and several other places in Spain; and, in 1706, the earl of Galway, at the head of 20,000 men, took Alcantara, a city of Portugal. In 1708, major-general Stanhope landed with 3000 men on the island of Minorca, and attacked fort St. Phillip, where the garrison, which consisted of 1000 Spaniards, and 600 French, surrendered in three days; the men were made pri-

soners

soners of war, and the whole island was conquered in three weeks.

These wars were concluded by the treaty of Utrecht, in 1713, by which Spain and Spanish America were confirmed to king Philip; but the Netherlands, and the Spanish dominions in Italy, were separated from that monarchy. Their Italian dominions consisted of the kingdoms of Naples, Sicily, Sardinia, and the duchy of Milan; of which, Naples, Sardinia, and Milan, were bestowed on the emperor; and Sicily, with the title of king, was given to the duke of Savoy. The Dutch had a barrier given them against France in the Netherlands; while Harley and Bolingbroke, the new ministry, in compliance to France, only insisted on the demolition of Dunkirk, and the possession of Gibraltar, Minorca, and Nova Scotia, though much better terms had before been offered by the French. Queen Anne procured a law for the rebuilding fifty new churches within the bills of mortality, with an augmentation of the livings of the poor clergy; and, in 1706, the union of the two kingdoms of England and Scotland took place. The queen died at Kensington, on the 1st of August, 1714, in the 50th year of her age, and the 13th of her reign. She had been married to his royal highness prince George of Denmark, July 28, 1683, by whom

whom she had several children, who died young.

Anne Stuart, queen of Great Britain, was in her person of a middle size, majestic, and well proportioned. Her hair was of a dark brown colour, her complexion ruddy, her features regular, and her countenance round and handsome. Her voice was clear and melodious, and her presence engaging. She was indeed deficient in that vigour of mind by which a prince ought to preserve his independence, and avoid the snares of sycophants and favorites: but, whatever her weakness in this particular might have been, the virtues of her heart were never called in question. She was a pattern of conjugal affection and fidelity, a tender mother, a warm friend, and indulgent mistress, a munificent patroness, and a merciful princess, during whose reign no subject's blood was shed for treason. In a word, if she was not the greatest, she was certainly one of the best and most unblemished sovereigns that ever sat upon the throne of England.

Remarkable Events in this Reign.

1703. Nov. 3. The most terrible storm that had ever been known in England.

1706. The kingdoms of England and Scotland united.

1707. Oct. 24. The first British parliament met.

1710.

1710. The cathedral church of St. Paul, London, rebuilt.

GEORGE I.

GEORGE I. was created duke of Cambridge, October 6, 1706, and on the death of queen Anne succeeded to the crown of Great Britain. He was the eldest son of Ernestus Augustus, duke, afterwards elector, of Brunswick-Lunenburgh (or Hanover,) by the princess Sophia, daughter of Frederick, elector-palatine, and king of Bohemia, and of Elizabeth, eldest daughter of James I. He was born May 28, 1660, and succeeded his father as elector of Brunswick-Lunenburgh, in 1698. The regency met, and gave orders immediately for his proclamation. On September 18, he landed, with the prince his son, at Greenwich, and on the 20th they made their public entry through the city to St. James's, attended by above 200 coaches and six of the nobility and gentry. The prince royal was declared prince of Wales; the king was crowned October 20; and a new parliament met on March 17, 1715. In July the king gave the royal assent to an act for preventing tumults and riotous assemblies, commonly called the Riot-Act, which is still in force.

This

This year a rebellion broke out which was headed by the earl of Mar in Scotland, who set up the pretender's standard, in September, in the Highlands, and caused him to be proclaimed in several places; when the earl of Derwentwater, and others, appeared in arms in the North of England, and proclaimed the pretender in several places. On November 12, they were attacked by the king's troops, commanded by the generals, Wills and Carpenter, in Preston, where, after a smart firing from the windows, finding all the avenues to the town blocked up, by the king's troops, on the 13th they desired to capitulate; but, no other terms being allowed them, than submitting to the king's mercy, on the 14th, at seven in the morning, they submitted. On the very day the rebels were subdued at Preston, the duke of Argyle defeated the rebel army, under the earl of Mar, consisting of about 8 or 9000 men, at Sheriff-muir, about four miles from Aberdeen; and the earl of Mar retreated to Perth, after an obstinate fight, in which both sides claimed the victory, though the earl being frustrated in his design of crossing the Forth, showed that the king's forces had the advantage. On December 22, the Pretender arrived in a Dunkirk privateer in Scotland, where he was met and complimented by the earl of Mar, and others of his adherents; but, being

closely

closely pursued by the king's troops, on February 14, the pretender, with the earl of Mar, and some chiefs, found means to make their escape to a French ship which lay there : soon after which the rebels were conducted into the mountains by Gordon, their general, where they dispersed. Some submitted, and some were taken prisoners. Among them was their general Forster, as also the earls of Derwentwater, Nithisdale, Darnwarth, Wintoun, and other noblemen. The lords Derwentwater and Kenmuir were beheaded on Tower-hill, February 24, 1715-16; Nithisdale and Wintoun made their escape out of the Tower; and after the execution of some of the rebels, an act of grace passed. Robert Walpole, esq. was some time before made first commissioner of the treasury, and chancellor of the exchequer; and about the same time, the parliament attainted James Butler, duke of Ormond, of high treason, and confiscated his estate. A few weeks after the king gave the royal assent to an act for enlarging the time of continuance of parliament for seven, instead of three years, as by the triennial act passed in the reign of king William.

A quadruple alliance was signed at London, July 22, 1718, between the emperor, Great Britain, and Holland. On July 31, Sir George Byng entirely defeated the Spanish fleet in the Mediterranean, the Spaniards
having

having attacked the citadel of Messina in Sicily, which was agreed to be given up to the emperor. War was declared against Spain in December following, both by Great Britain and France.

' The year 1720 was remarkable for the South Sea scheme, when the greatest part of the nation turned stock-jobbers. South Sea Stock rose and fell till it came to above 1000; but it fell faster than it rose, and many families were ruined by it, while a few got vast riches. The directors' estates were sold for the benefit of the sufferers, and they were incapacitated from sitting in either house of parliament, or holding any office or place of trust for ever. Sir Robert Walpole, who had resigned, was again made chancellor of the exchequer, and first lord of the treasury; which post he held to the end of this reign, and fifteen years after.

On the 15th of April, 1721, the princess of Wales was delivered of William Augustus, the famous duke of Cumberland. A new parliament met on Oct. 2, 1722, when the king acquainted them with a conspiracy for overturning the established government, and setting up the pretender. Christopher Layer, a counsellor of the Temple, was executed at Tyburn, May 17, 1723, and his head fixed upon Temple-bar, for being concerned in it. The parliament passed bills for inflicting pains and penalties on bishops Atterbury, Kelley,

Kelley, and Plunket, on the same account, whereby the first was banished, and the two last imprisoned for life. In 1725, the earl of Macclesfield, lord high chancellor, resigned the seals; he was fined 30,000l. and committed to the Tower till he paid it. He was succeeded by Sir Peter King, lord chief justice of the common pleas. At this time was passed an act for regulating elections in the city of London. The same session, Henry St. John, lord Viscount Bolingbroke, was restored to his estates, and an act passed for that purpose, though he was not restored to his title. In the same year, the order of the Bath was revived, and 37 new knights were installed.

On Sept. 3, 1725, a treaty was concluded between Great Britain, France, and Prussia; though the last, in effect, soon deserted this alliance; but the States-general afterwards acceded to it. This treaty was designed as a balance to one which had been concluded between the courts of Vienna and Madrid. These counter-alliances put Europe again in a flame, and three British squadrons were fitted out; one sent to the West Indies, another to the coast of Spain, and a third to the Baltic. In the beginning of the year 1727, the Spaniards laid siege to Gibraltar; which, though it was suspended upon preliminary articles for a general pacification being signed, was not ratified till some time

after

after the king's death.   On June 3, his majesty embarked on board the Carolina yacht,
and landed on the 7th at Vaert in Holland,
where he lay that night.   On the 9th he
arrived at Delden, between 11 and 12 at
night, seemingly in good health.   He set out
the next morning about 3 o'clock, was taken
ill on the road, and died at his brother's palace at Osnaburgh, June 11, 1727, in the
68th year of his age, and the 13th of his
reign.

George I. was plain and simple in his person and address; grave and composed in his
deportment, though easy, familiar and facetious, in his hours of relaxation.   Before he
ascended the throne of Great Britain, he had
acquired the character of a circumspect general, a just and merciful prince, and a wise
politician, who perfectly understood, and
steadily pursued his own interest.   With these
qualities, it cannot be doubted but that he
came to England extremely well disposed to
govern his new subjects according to the
maxims of the British constitution, and the
genius of the people; and if ever he seemed
to deviate from these principles, we may take
it for granted, that he was misled by the
venal suggestions of a ministry, whose power
and influence were founded on corruption.

Remarkable

Remarkable Events in this Reign.

1715. April 22. A total eclipse.
1727. Inoculation first tried on criminals with success.

Russia, formerly a dukedom, established as an empire.

GEORGE II.

GEORGE II. (then in the 44th year of his age) was proclaimed king of Great Britain, on the 15th of June, 1727, being the day after the express arrived with the account of the death of his father. On the 11th of October, the coronation of the king and queen was performed at Westminster-abbey, with the usual solemnity.

In the beginning of December, his majesty's eldest son, prince Frederick, arrived in England, from Hanover, where he had hitherto resided: he was introduced into the privy council, and created prince of Wales.

The Spaniards still continued their depredations with impunity on the commerce of Great Britain. The court of Spain indeed, at this juncture, seemed cold and indifferent with regard to a pacification with England. In September, 1729, Victor Amadeus, king of Sardinia, resigned his crown to his son,

M 2   Charles

Charles Emanuel, prince of Piedmont. The father reserved to himself a revenue of 100,000 pistoles per annum, retired to the castle of Chamberry, and espoused the countess dowager of St. Sebastian.

On the 1st of Feb. 1773, died Augustus II. king of Poland, which gave rise to a dreadful war in Europe. Three parties were formed on this occasion.

1734, king Stanislaus was obliged to flee secretly from Dantzic, and leave the crown of Poland to Augustus, elector of Saxony. England during these transactions preserved a neutrality. At length, a quarrel breaking out between the courts of Madrid and Lisbon, the latter applied for assistance to the king of Great Britain, who sent Sir John Norris with a powerful squadron to Lisbon.

On the 27th of April, 1736, the prince of Wales was married to the princess of Saxe-Gotha.

The beginning of the year 1737 was distinguished by a rupture in the royal family, occasioned by the prince of Wales carrying away the princess of Wales, then near her time, from Hampton-court, where their majesties resided, to St. James's, where she was that night delivered of Augusta, now princess of Brunswick. On the 20th of November died queen Caroline, in the 55th year of her age. The dissension still subsisted between the prince of Wales and his father, who ordered

the

the lord chamberlain to signify publicly, that no person who visited the prince should be admitted to the court at St. James's. In 1739 war was declared against Spain, and admiral Vernon sent in July, with a squadron of ships, to annoy their commerce and settlements in America; where, in November, he took the town of Porto Bello, with only six ships. The next year advice was received from admiral Vernon, that he had bombarded Carthagena, and taken Fort Chagre. On the 20th of October, Charles VI. emperor of Germany, the last prince of the house of Austria, died at Vienna, and was succeeded in his hereditary dominions by his eldest daughter, the archduchess Maria Theresa. The young king of Prussia was no sooner informed of the emperor's death, than he entered Silesia at the head of 20,000 men and seized certain fiefs, to which his family laid claim. The elector of Bavaria refused to acknowledge the archduchess as queen of Hungary and Bohemia.

The year 1747 was remarkable for general Wentworth and admiral Vernon's unsuccessful expedition against Carthagena, owing to a disagreement which arose between them.

By the happy influence of his Britannic majesty a treaty was concluded between Austria and Prussia, whereby Silesia was given up to the latter; to which treaty Saxony also acceded, and peace was proclaimed at Dresden, on

the

the 17th of September, 1742. This obliged the French to retire with great precipitation and loss to Prague, which prince Charles besieged with 60,000 men, there being 26,000 men in that city. Negociations were carried on between the generals on the respective sides. The British fleet, under Sir Chaloner Ogle, was no ways fortunate in America. Commodore Knowles was sent out with a squadron of ships to attack La Guirre and Porto Cavello, on the coast of Caraccas; but this attempt miscarried. He afterwards attacked Porto Cavallo, but without success.

The queen of Hungary now began to triumph over all her enemies: the French were driven out of Bohemia, and prince Charles, her general, at the head of a large army, invaded the dominions of Bavaria. The elector was obliged to fly before her: and abandoned by his allies, and stripped of all his dominions, he repaired to Frankfort, where he lived in indigence and obscurity. He now made advances towards an accommodation with the queen of Hungary; and agreed to continue neuter during the remainder of the war, while the French, who first began it as allies, supported the burthen. In the Netherlands, the English and French armies came to an engagement at the village of Dettingen, June 26, 1743. The order of battle, as directed by his Britannic majesty,

was

was very masterly. The king advancing to
the front of his army, gave fresh spirits to
the soldiers. The British troops fired too
soon upon the marching up of the enemy ;
when the French black musquetaires, de-
taching themselves from their lines, and gal-
loping between the allied foot, were all cut
to pieces. The firing now became general ;
when the presence of his Britannic majesty, who was in the posts of the greatest
danger, and behaved with the noblest intrepidity, fixed the fate of the day. Marshal Noailles showed great bravery in this
battle. The duke of Cumberland being in
the hottest of the engagement, was wounded
in the calf of his leg. Hereupon Marshal
Noailles, after losing the flower of his army,
ordered a retreat. In this battle the French
lost 6000 men, and a multitude of officers,
with some trophies ; and the English 2500
men.

In 1744, commodore Anson returned from
his expedition round the world. The French
went on with vigor in every quarter ; they
opposed prince Charles of Lorraine ; interrupted his progress in his attempt to pass the
Rhine, and gained some success in Italy ;
but their chief expectations were placed in
a projected invasion of England. The troops
designed for this expedition amounted to
15,000. The duke de Roquefeuille, with
twenty ships of the line, was to see them
landed

landed safely in England; and count Saxe was to command them, when put ashore. The whole project, however, was disconcerted by the appearance of Sir John Norris, with a superior fleet, making up against them; the French fleet was obliged to put back; a very hard gale of wind damaged their transports beyond redress. All hopes of invasion were now frustrated; and, at length, the French thought fit openly to declare war. The combined fleets of France and Spain for some time, fought the British armament under the Admirals Matthews and Lestock, though with inferior force, and came off nearly upon equal terms. Such a parity of success in England was regarded as a defeat. Both the English admirals were tried by a court-martial; Matthews, who had fought the enemy with intrepidity, was declared incapable of serving for the future in his majesty's navy; Lestock, who had kept aloof, was acquitted with honor, as he had intrenched himself within the punctilios of discipline; he barely did his duty: a man of honor, when his country is at stake, should do more. The proceedings in the Netherlands were still more unfavourable. The French besieged and took Friberg, before they went into winter quarters; and early the next campaign, invested the city of Tournay. The allies were resolved to prevent the loss of this city by a battle. Their

army

army was inferior to the French; notwithstanding this disadvantage, on the 30th of April, 1745, the duke of Cumberland marched to the attack at two in the morning. The British infantry pressed forward, bore down all opposition, and for near an hour, were victorious. Marshal Saxe was at that time sick of the same disorder of which he afterwards died. He visited all the posts in a litter; and saw, notwithstanding all appearances, that the day was his own. The English column, without command, by a mere mechanical courage, had advanced upon the enemy's lines, which formed an avenue on each side to receive them. The French artillery began to play upon this forlorn body; and though they continued a long time unshaken, they were obliged to retreat about three o'clock in the afternoon. The allies left near 12,000 men upon the field of battle, and the French bought their victory with almost an equal number. This blow by which Tournay was taken, gave the French a manifest superiority during the continuance of the war.

The son of the old pretender now resolved to make an effort at gaining the British crown. Being furnished with some money, and still larger promises from France, he embarked for Scotland on board a small frigate, accompanied by the Marquis Tullbardine, and a few other desperate adventurers. For the conquest of the whole British empire, he brought with him seven officers, and arms for 2000 men. He landed on the coast of Lochabar, July 27, and was in a little time joined by some Highland chiefs, and their vassals. He soon saw himself at the head of 1500 men, and invited others to join him by manifestoes, which were dispersed throughout all the highlands. The ministry was no sooner informed of the truth of his arrival, than Sir John Cope was ordered to oppose his progress. In the mean time, the young adventurer marched to Perth, where his father, the chevalier de St. George, was proclaimed king of Great Britain. The rebel army advanced towards Edinburgh, which they entered without opposition. Here too the pageantry of proclamation was performed. But, though he was master of the capital, yet the citadel or castle, with a good garrison, under the command of General Guest, braved all his attempts. Sir John Cope, who was now reinforced by two regiments of dragoons, resolved to march towards Edinburgh, and give him battle. The young adventurer attacked him near Preston Pans, and in a few minutes totally routed him and his troops. In this victory the king lost about 500 men, and the rebels not above 80.

In the mean time, the pretender went forward with vigour; and having advanced to Penrith, continued his irruption till he

came

came to Manchester, where he established his head-quarters; from thence he prosecuted his route to Derby; but he determined once more to return to Scotland. He effected his retreat to Carlisle, without any loss, and, having reinforced the garrison of the place, crossed the rivers Eden and Solway into Scotland.

After many attacks and skirmishes, the duke of Cumberland put himself at the head of the troops at Edinburgh, which consisted of about 14,000 men. He resolved to come to a battle as soon as possible, and marched forward while the young adventurer retired at his approach. The duke advanced to Aberdeen; where he was joined by the duke of Gordon, and some other lords. The Highlanders were drawn up in order of battle, on the plain of Culloden, to the number of 8000 men. The duke marched thither, and the battle began about one o'clock in the afternoon, April 16. In less than thirty minutes, the rebels were totally routed, and the field was covered with their dead bodies. The duke, immediately after the battle, ordered thirty-six deserters to be executed. At length, a general peace was proclaimed in London, on February 2, 1749.

On the 7th of May, 1756, his Britannic majesty declared war against France, and sent admiral Byng, with a strong fleet, to the relief of Minorca; but as he neglected to fulfil

fulfil his instructions, the place was lost, and he was tryed and shot at Portsmouth. During these transactions, Mr. Clive, one of the clerks of the East India Company, distinguished himself in the East Indies, obtaining the rank of colonel, and had such amazing success, that all the towns and factories of the French on the coast of Coromandel, except Pondicherry, were, in a few years, taken by the English. On the other hand in 1758, the duke of Marlborough landed near St. Maloes in France, and burnt many ships with a great quantity of naval stores. Lieutenant-general Bligh and Captain Howe took Cherburg, and demolished the fortifications. Soon after, Captain Marsh took Senegal, and commodore Keppel, the island of Goree on the coast of Africa. On the 26th of July, Cape Breton was retaken by General Amherst and Admiral Boscawen. Soon after, fort Frontenac surrendered to Lieutenant General Bradstreet, and fort du Quesne to general Forbes. On the 1st of May, 1759, the island of Guadaloupe surrendered to the English. In the same month, Marigalante, Santos, and Deseada, became subject to Great Britain.

On August 1, was fought the glorious battle of Minden, in which about 7000 English defeated 80,000 of the French regular troops.

The command of the expedition against
Quebec

Quebec, the capital of French Canada, was given to general Wolfe, a young officer of a true military genius. Wolfe's courage and perseverance surmounted incredible difficulties; he gained the heights of Abraham, near Quebec, where he fought and defeated the French army, but he was himself killed. General Amherst, who was the first English general on command in America, conducted another expedition; and Canada shortly became subject to Great Britain.

The affairs of the French being now desperate, and their credit ruined, they resolved upon an attempt to retrieve all by an invasion of Great Britain ; but, on the 18th of August, 1759, admiral Boscawen attacked the Toulon squadron, commanded by M. de la Clue, near the Straits of Gibraltar, took three ships and burnt two.

On the 20th of November, Sir Edward Hawke defeated the Brest fleet, commanded by admiral Conflans, off the island of Dumet, in the bay of Biscay. After this engagement, the French gave over all thoughts of their intended invasion of Great Britain.

In February, 1760, captain Thurot, a French marine adventurer, who with three sloops of war had alarmed the coasts of Scotland, and actually made a descent at Carrickfergus, in Ireland, was, on his return from thence, defeated, and killed, by captain Elliot, who was the commodore of three ships inferior in force to the Frenchmen's squadron.

On the 26th of October, 1760, George II. died suddenly, full of years and glory, in the 77th year of his age, and the 33d of his reign. He was interred on the 10th of November, at Westminster.

George II. was rather low of stature, well shaped and erect, with eyes remarkably prominent, a high nose, and fair complexion. In his disposition, he is said to have been hasty, prone to anger, especially in his youth, yet soon appeased; otherwise mild, moderate, and humane; in his way of living, temperate and regular. He was fond of military pomp and parade, and personally brave. He loved war as a soldier; studied it as a science, and corresponded on the subject with some of the greatest military characters in Germany. The circumstances that chiefly mark his public character were a predilection for his native country, and a close attention to the political interests of the Germanic body.

Remarkable Events in this Reign.

1738. Westminster-bridge begun this year, and finished in 1750.

1753. The British Museum established.

1755. Lisbon destroyed by an earthquake.

1756. 123 Englishmen perished in the black hole at Calcutta.

1760.

1760. Blackfriars-bridge begun, and finished in 1770.

❧❧❧❧❧❧

GEORGE III.

GEORGE III. the eldest son of Frederick prince of Wales, was born on the 4th of June, 1738, and proclaimed king of Great Britain on the 26th of October, 1760. The brighter the national glory was at the time of George the Second's death, the more arduous was the province of his successor. This prince chose for his first minister the earl of Bute, with whom he had been acquainted from his earliest youth; and the first acts of his reign convinced the public, that the death of his predecessor would not relax the operations of the war. Accordingly, in 1761, the island of Belleisle, on the coast of France, surrendered to his majesty's ships and forces under commodore Keppel and general Hodgson; as did the important fortress of Pondicherry, in the East Indies, to general Coote and admiral Stevens. The operations against the French West Indies still continued, under general Monckton, lord Rollo, and Sir James Douglas; and in 1762, the island of Martinico, hitherto deemed impregnable, with the islands of Grenada, Grenadillas, St. Vincent, and

N 2   others

others of less note, were subdued by the British arms, with inconceivable rapidity: By this time the famous family compact among all the branches of the Bourbon family had been concluded; and it was found necessary to declare war against Spain, who, having been hitherto no principal in the quarrel, had scandalously abused their neutrality in favour of the French. A respectable armament was fitted out under admiral Pocock, having the earl of Albemarle on board to command the land forces; and the vitals of the Spanish monarchy were struck at by the reduction of the Havannah, the strongest and most important fort which his catholic majesty held in the West Indies. The capture of the Hermione, a large Spanish register ship, bound from Lima to Cadiz, the cargo of which was valued at a million sterling, preceded the birth of the prince of Wales, and the treasure passed in triumph through Westminster to the Bank the very hour he was born. The loss of the Havannah, with the ships and treasures there taken from the Spaniards, was succeeded by the reduction of Manilla, in the East Indies, by general Draper and admiral Cornish, with the capture of the Trinidad, reckoned worth three millions of dollars. To counteract those dreadful blows given to the family compact, the French and Spaniards opened their last resource, which was to

quarrel

quarrel with and invade Portugal, which had been always under the peculiar protection of the British arms. Whether this quarrel was real or pretended, is not for us to determine. It certainly embarrassed his Britannic majesty, who was obliged to send thither armaments both by sea and land; but these found no great difficulty in checking the progress of the Spaniards. The enemy, at last, granted such terms as the British ministry thought admissible, and adequate to the occasion. A cessation of arms took place in Germany, and in all other quarters; and on the 10th of February, 1763, the definitive treaty of peace between his Britannic majesty, the king of France, and the king of Spain, was concluded at Paris, and acceded to by the king of Portugal. The ratifications were exchanged at Paris, on the 10th of March: on the 22d of the same month, peace was solemnly proclaimed at the usual places in Westminster and London; and the treaty, having been laid before the parliament, met with the approbation of a majority of both houses.

In the East Indies, in 1764, the nabob, set up by lord Clive, was deposed; and the factory not agreeing with the nabob's successor, 4000 of the garrison and inhabitants of Patna were put to the sword, and the town plundered, besides several of the English being surprised and cut to pieces.

Upon

Upon these and other acts of hostility, war was declared against the nabob, Cossim Ali Cawn; and the former nabob, Meer Jaffier, was soon restored, who, thereupon entered into a more advantageous treaty with the company. Soon after, an action happened, in which the English were victorious. After this success, the city of Moorshedabad became an easy conquest; and, not long after, the restored nabob, Meer Jaffier, was proclaimed. In the mean time, the French took possession of Turk's Island, and of nine sail of English ships: they then destroyed every house, and secured all the slaves they could find. Major Adams, however, the English commander, again routed the enemy, and carried Rajamoul by assault, when Patna soon surrendered.

In 1766, peace was established in the East Indies by lord Clive, who returned the following year; but a new enemy now started up, Hyder Ally, who, from a common soldier, had become a prince of a large tract of territory, on the Malabar coast, in confederacy with the viceroy of the Decan, declared war against the English. The council of Madras sent a body of troops under Colonel Smith who obtained a complete victory over them, when the viceroy immediately made peace with the English. Hyder Ally took refuge among the mountains, from whence he made frequent incursions. In 1768, a

small

small fleet forced into Mangalore, one of Hyder's principal sea-ports, and carried off his fleet. This war continued till the next year, when peace was proposed to Hyder, and accepted. Having thus finished the affairs of the East, we must return to the transactions at home.

During the administration of Mr. Grenville, in 1765, bills passed for laying a stamp-duty on the British colonies in America, which first laid the foundation of those quarrels between the colonies and the mother country, which ended in a total separation. This measure was no sooner known in America, than insurrections commenced there, and great murmurings at home. In consequence of which the ministry retired, and the act was repealed.

In the course of this year, the sovereignty of the Isle of Man was annexed to the crown of England; and on account of the seizure of Mr. Wilkes's papers, general warrants granted by secretaries of state, except in cases of high-treason, were declared to be illegal and oppressive.

The next year, several changes in the ministry took place; the duke of Grafton was appointed first lord of the treasury, and Mr. Pitt, who had been created earl of Chatham, was made lord privy seal; but lord North was soon after placed at the head of administration.

Mr.

Mr. Wilkes, who had long resided abroad, returned in 1768, and offered himself as a candidate to represent the city of London, though a sentence of outlawry against him had never been repealed. He lost his election ; but immediately stood for Middlesex, where he was chosen by a great majority. He soon after surrendered himself, and was committed to the King's Bench prison. In consequence of which, several riots happened in St. George's Fields, and some persons were killed. The ministry determined to persecute Mr. Wilkes, who was accordingly expelled the house of commons, fined a thousand pounds, and imprisoned two and twenty months, for publishing No. 45, of the North Britain, the Essay on Woman, and some other papers. This severity only increased Mr. Wilkes's popularity, who was several times elected for Middlesex, till it was resolved, that Mr. Luttrell, who had opposed him, but had not one third as many votes, ought to have been returned. Petitions were presented from various quarters, complaining that the rights of election were infringed, and a general discontent prevailed.

Mr. Wilkes's imprisonment expired in 1771, when he was chosen one of the sheriffs for London and Middlesex, made an alderman, had his debts paid, amounting to twenty or thirty thousand pounds, was elected

ed lord mayor, and afterwards chamberlain of London.

While matters were in this situation at home, they were getting much worse in America, where the joy which the repeal of the stamp-act had occasioned, was of short duration. New duties were laid on paper, glass, tea, and other articles ; but as a general combination seemed forming not to take any of those commodities from the mother country, the acts were repealed, except the duties on tea. Laws were also passed which gave great umbrage, for quartering troops in America, for suspending the legislative power at New York, and for appointing governors in the colonies who were to be paid by the crown. Some vessels laden with tea attempted to land in America; but at Boston and South Carolina the teas were thrown into the sea, and from other places the ships returned with their cargoes untouched. These proceedings enraged the government of England, which passed acts for shutting up the port of Boston, and for altering the constitution of Massachusetts Bay and Quebec, so that the magistrates might be appointed by the king of England.

In this situation of affairs, the Americans entered into an agreement not to trade with Great Britain till these acts were repealed. At the same time, the delegates appointed from the English colonies, avowed their loyalty

alty to his majesty, but supplicated him to
order a change of measures.   This petition of
the congress was rejected, and the application of their agents to be heard at the bar
of the House of Commons was refused, and
finally a bill of the earl of Chatham's, to
accommodate the troubles of America, was
rejected in the House of Lords.

The Americans, finding themselves thus
treated, began to train their militia with
great industry.   They erected powder-mills
in Philadelphia and Virginia, and began to
prepare arms in all the provinces; nor were
these preparations fruitless, as will evidently
appear from what followed.   On the 19th
of April, 1775, general Gage detached a
party to seize some military stores at Con-
cord, in New England.   Several skirmishes
ensued, many were killed on both sides, and
the troops would probably have been all cut
off if a fresh body had not arrived to their
relief.   Arms were now taken up in every
quarter, and they assumed the title of, *The
United Colonies of America.*   The first resolutions were for raising an army, for establishing an extensive paper currency, and
for stopping all exportations to those places
which still retained their obedience.   About
240 provincials next took the garrison of
Ticonderago and Crown Point, without any
loss of men; and here they found plenty of
military stores.   Great Britain increased
her

her army, and sent over the generals Howe, Burgoyne, and Clinton.

These inimical proceedings did not terrify the congress, who encouraged the people of Massachusetts Bay to resume their chartered rights, ordered the blockade of Boston to be discontinued; and, that they might secure Charles-town, in one night they raised very considerable works on Bunker's hill. As soon as they were discovered in the morning, a heavy fire ensued from the ships, the floating batteries, and from Cop's-hill in Boston. This they sustained, and were with difficulty driven from their entrenchments in the evening by a large party, under the conduct of the generals Howe and Pigot. The contest was severe, Charles-town was burned, 226 of the English officers and men were killed. The Americans then threw up works on the other side of Charles-town neck; so that the troops were as closely invested as they had been at Boston.

George Washington, esq. was, about this time, appointed to the command of the American army; the congress published spirited memorials of their reasons for taking up arms, and offered a second fruitless petition to the king. Their generals were then ordered to endeavour to subjugate those colonies that espoused the cause of Great Britain. Two parties were sent against Canada, under general Montgomery and colonel B. Arnold,

nold, who boldly undertook to march by an untried route, from Boston to Quebec. After innumerable difficulties, they reached the town, which they first attempted to take by storm, and then to block up. In this attempt, Montgomery fell, and Arnold, who was dangerously wounded, was forced to make a hasty retreat. In the mean time, general Carlton, the governor of Canada, received fresh supplies from England.

In 1776, Boston was bombarded and evacuated; when general Washington took possession of it, and general Howe removed his troops to Halifax. While the breach was thus widening in America, several members of the British senate were at home endeavouring to bring matters to a reconciliation, but it was not the disposition of the reigning ministry to give up any thing that they apprehended could promote their wild and chimerical schemes.

In July, a fruitless attack was made upon Charles-town, in which the English suffered considerably. About this time, general Howe landed and drove the Americans out of Long Island, who abandoned New York to the British forces. Offers of reconciliation were now made by Howe, and rejected. Sir Peter Parker and general Clinton took Rhode Island, and the English also made some incursions into the Jerseys. General Washington, soon after, surprised and took
prisoners

prisoners above 900 of the Hessian troops in our service, with several stands of arms. Privateers were also fitted out from England and America, who continually made prizes of each other, and matters were carried on with great animosity on both sides.

The next year, there were two actions between the generals Howe and Washington, and Philadelphia surrendered to the king's troops. A plan was now formed for invading the revolted colonies by way of Canada, and General Burgoyne undertook the expedition; but after many difficulties, and some desperate actions, this army was obliged to surrender themselves prisoners of war to Gates and Arnold. Our expedition up the North river was more successful, under Clinton and Vaughan; the former of whom, soon after, succeeded general Howe as commander in chief; and, after evacuating Philadelphia, he retreated with his army to New York.

In 1778, the French entered into an alliance with the thirteen United Colonies; and as affairs wore so gloomy an aspect, the earl of Carlisle, William Eden, and George Johnstone, esqrs. were sent as commissioners to treat of peace; but the hour was past, and the terms were rejected with disdain. The war was then carried on with mutual animosity, and the whole of Georgia was reduced by the British forces. Hostilities next

o

commenced

commenced with France; and the English admiral Keppel engaged the French fleet under Count D'Orvilliers. Not a ship was taken on either side; and, upon some censure being passed on vice admiral Sir Hugh Palliser's conduct, he applied to Keppel for redress, which was denied. He then exhibited articles of accusation against Keppel, who was tried and honorably acquitted. Palliser was next tried, and acquitted, and there the farce ended.

In the mean time, Sir Edward Vernon, in the East Indies, drove off the French under De Tronjolly; and, soon after, Pondicherry surrendered to the arms of England, as did St. Lucia in the West Indies. Dominica, St. Vincent, and Grenada, however, were taken by the French, who, in 1779, assisted the Americans with a fleet under Count D'Estaing. But general Prevost repulsed the Americans and their allies at Savannah, and the latter were soon obliged to abandon the enterprize. In this year, the French made an unsuccessful attempt on the island of Jersey; and, some time after, Sir Hyde Parker took several of their ships. Spain now joined France against us, took New Orleans, on the Mississippi, and laid siege to Gibraltar with great ardor. The combined fleets of France and Spain rode triumphant in the Channel, but separated without effecting any thing.

Sir

Sir G. B. Rodney, in the beginning of 1780, with a large fleet, captured seven vessels, and, a few days afterwards, captured five Spanish ships of the line; one was lost by being driven on shore, and another was blown up. In April and May, the same admiral, after throwing supplies into Gibraltar, had three undecisive engagements with the French fleet in the West Indies, where several of our ships suffered dreadfully in a hurricane, and some were lost. In July, admiral Geary took twelve French merchant ships; but the combined fleet in August took five English East-Indiamen, and fifty merchant ships bound for the West-Indies.

In America, general Clinton took possession of Charles-town; earl Cornwallis obtained a victory over general Gates, and colonel Tarleton acquired fame by his conduct in several skirmishes. In July, a fleet, and a large body of troops from France, arrived at Rhode Island.

This year was remarkable for one of the most dreadful riots that ever happened in the city and suburbs of London. An association of Protestant sectaries, with lord George Gordon at their head, alarmed themselves with fancied apprehensions of popery, and determined to excite the legislature to repeal an act they had just passed in favor of the catholics. A petition was accordingly signed by above 100,000 persons, and presented

with

with due decorum to the house of Commons
on the 2d of June, but in the course of the
day, several lords and commoners were insulted by the mob.   The Sardinian and other
Romish chapels were pulled down; and
such other outrages were committed that it
was found expedient to draw out the military,
and to send five of the rioters to Newgate.
Every thing remained quiet on the king's
birth-day, which was kept on Saturday instead of Sunday, on which day another Popish chapel was demolished.   On Monday,
the 5th, a Popish school, three priests'
houses, a library, and all Sir George Sa-
ville's furniture, were destroyed.   On Tues-
day, the mob was so riotous, before both
houses of parliament, that they obliged
them to adjourn; and in the evening, when
the keeper of Newgate refused to deliver up
the rioters, they set fire to his house and the
prison, and let out about 300 prisoners, many
of whom joined them.   They then proceeded
to the Bank, which they would have plundered had it not been protected by the military
and city association.   In the evening, lord
Mansfield's, Mr. Langdale's house and distil-
lery, and Sir John Fielding's were burnt, and
several private persons had their houses pulled
down.   On the next day, the King's Bench
prison, the New Bridewell, the Fleet prison,
some Popish chapels, and several Papists'
houses were destroyed.   Fires were seen
blazing

blazing in every part of the capital, and the lawless mob were exacting contributions from the citizens, while the magistrates, and even the ministry viewed these scenes of desolation with an inactivity that was astonishing. At length, however, their courage seemed roused, troops were called into London from all quarters, and were stationed in every part of the town. This step effectually checked the progress of the rioters, a great number of whom were shot by the military, and others taken, tried, and executed. Lord George Gordon was also tried, but acquitted.

During these disturbances, a rupture was expected with the Dutch, who had for some time past privately assisted the Americans. In January, commodore Fielding took several ships with naval stores on board, which were under convoy of the Dutch admiral; and, in September, Keppel captured a congress packet boat, on board of which was Mr. Lawrens, late president of the congress, among whose papers was found the plan of a treaty between America and Holland. Mr. Lawrens was committed to the Tower, and fresh applications were made to the States General; but, as no satisfactory answer could be obtained, hostilities were declared by the English, on Dec. 20, 1780.

In September, this year, the Resolution and Discovery returned from a voyage round the world; but neither of their commanders, the captains Cook and Clerk, returned with them. The former was unfortunately killed by the natives of Owhyhee, a newly discovered island, on the 14th of Feb. 1770, and the latter died, soon after, of a consumption.

In 1781, intelligence was brought to England, that our shipping had suffered considerably by several hurricanes, in the Leeward Islands, which did incredible damage at land and sea. The war with Holland began vigorously. Admiral Rodney and general Vaughan took the islands of St. Eustatius, St. Martin, Seba, and St. Bartholomew, with a Dutch flag ship of 60 guns, a frigate of 38, and above 200 smaller vessels. However, we did not long enjoy the former part of this victory; for, before the close of the year, St. Eustatius, by some unaccountable misconduct, was taken by the French; and the Dutch colonies of Demerara and Issequibo surrendered to admiral Rodney. Commodore Johnstone took four Dutch East-Indiamen in the bay of Saldannah, where a fifth was burned; and admiral H. Parker had a very severe engagement with the Dutch fleet off the Dogger Bank. One of the enemy's ships sunk in the night, but none were taken.

Our army in America still continued their operations with different success. Fort Anne and Fort George surrendered to general Carleton. Great expectations were now formed from

from the discontent of some rebel troops, and the Pennsylvania line; but all attempts on our part, to induce them to join the royal army proved fruitless. Admiral Arbuthnot engaged the French fleet in America, and assisted the generals Phipps and Arnold in ravaging Virginia. Skirmishes were frequent; but earl Cornwallis, by rapid marches, prevented the junction of the rebel armies. On the other hand, a party under colonel Tarleton suffered much in an engagement with general Morgan. In the mean time, Wilmington surrendered to the royal arms, and some batteries were destroyed. Earl Cornwallis gained a victory over general Green, near Guildford, in North Carolina; and a second engagement with lord Rawdon followed. However, the day was now hastily arriving, in which Britain was to give up all hopes of ever conquering America; for soon after, De Grasse reached the Chesapeak; and, before admiral Graves could attack him, general Washington, with his assistance, surrounded earl Cornwallis's troops, who were obliged to surrender themselves prisoners of war to the combined forces of France and America.

About the same time, the Spaniards made themselves masters of Pensacola, and the whole of West Florida. They also pushed the siege of Gibraltar with great spirit; but a party of our troops made a sally from the
fortress,

fortress, and destroyed all their works, which were nearly completed.

The French dispatched their fleets to attempt distressing us in every quarter. They attacked Jersey; and the lieutenant-governor Cobbet was tried and suspended for his strange neglect of duty. M. de la Motte Piquett captured part of the St. Eustatia fleet; and another squadron attacked governer Johnstone, off St. Jago, when the action was severe, and the ships on both sides were much damaged. The French also landed at St. Lucia; but, without being able to accomplish any thing there, they quitted it, and proceeded to Tobago, which they obliged to capitulate.

In the East-Indies, soon after Sir Hector Monro had taken the field, a party under colonel Baily, attempting to join him, was either cut to pieces or taken by Hyder Ally, who took Arcot by assault, and obliged the fort to capitulate. The command of the company's troops was soon after given to Sir Eyre Coote, who obtained a complete victory over Ally, between Porto Novo and Mooteapallam. Some of Ally's ships also were burned on the Malabar coast by Sir Edward Hughes. Basan soon after surrendered; and colonel Carnac engaged and conquered Mhadage Scindia. The French then left the Coromandel coast without assisting Hyder Ally, who quitted the Carnatic.

Admiral

Admiral Rodney and general Vaughan made an unsuccessful attempt against St. Vincent's ; but admiral Kempenfelt was more fortunate in taking several transports, which were under convoy of the French fleet, commanded by M. de Guichen.

In the mean time, every action of the ministry at home was narrowly scrutinized by the minority, who were led by the hon. Mr. Fox and Mr. Burke. In the House of Peers the increase of popery, and the commutation of tythes, were canvassed. In the House of Commons, bills were brought in for regulating his majesty's civil establishment, for limiting the jurisdiction of the supreme court of Calcutta, and for other important purposes.

In 1782, after the surrender of earl Cornwallis, our war with America appeared desperate, and every one seemed desirous of bringing it to a conclusion, except those whose ambition or ignorance had been the cause of it. Sir James Lowther, (the late earl of Lonsdale) therefore moved, in the House of Commons, that all further attempts to reduce the Americans by force would be injurious to the true interests of Great Britain. After a long and vigorous debate, the motion was rejected. The mode of exchanging prisoners was next canvassed ; and Mr. Lawrens was ordered to be released from the Tower. A motion was next made for addressing

dressing his majesty to put a stop to the American war; and the motion was lost by one vote only. A second motion was then made and agreed to. Addresses were presented to the king, a complete change of administration followed, and the negociations for a general peace commenced. The independency of America was allowed. Some little skirmishes, however, took place: and the refugees, in British pay, after taking a fort on Tom's river, hanged the commander of it, to revenge some cruelties with which he was charged. This violently enraged the Americans, and general Washington demanded the officer who had condemned him, as a murderer. This was refused; on which captain Asgill, of the guards, was, by lot, ordered into confinement, and doomed to suffer in his stead. However, after a most painful suspense, he was released. His mother, lady Asgill, applied to the French minister, count de Vergennes, whose intercession with general Washington, strengthened by the generous interference of the queen of France, procured life and liberty to the unfortunate victim.

Sir Guy Carleton afterwards succeeded Sir Henry Clinton in the command. He immediately acquainted general Washington that admiral Digby and himself were empowered to treat of peace with the people of America; and, after the king's troops had evacuated Savannah,

vannah, the province of Georgia, and Charles-town, the provisional articles were signed at Paris, on the 30th of November. Thus terminated this inglorious war, in which so many valuable lives had been lost, and so many millions of money had been squandered away, to gratify the ambition of a few individuals, and to enrich some unprincipled contractors, who now bask in the sun-shine of affluence, at the expence of their country.

While matters were thus drawing to a crisis at home, Tanjour and Trichinopoly were delivered from the depredations of Hyder Ally. Intelligence also arrived, that general Coote had laid siege to Tripassore, and gained a second complete victory over Hyder's army. Sir Hector Monro, and Sir Edward Hughes, possesssed themselves of the Dutch settlement of Negapatam and Fort Ostenburg; Hyder's troops evacuated all their posts in the Tanjour; and several petty princes who had revolted, returned to their obedience. Sir Edward Hughes next took Trincomalee in the island of Ceylon, with two Dutch ships, and several small vessels. Major Abington relieved Tellicherry, which Hyder had besieged, and routed the enemy, taking from them 1500 prisoners, military stores, and treasure to a great amount. The French, however, with Hyder's son, Tippoo Saib, defeated the company's tioops soon after, and either captured or destroyed the

whole

whole detachment. Cuddalore also capitulated to the French. Hostilities afterwards
ceased between the Mahrattas and the company's forces; but M. Suffrein, with the
French fleet, coming to the assistance of
Hyder, took Permacoli. Several engagements followed between admiral Hughes and
Suffrein, some of which were desperate, but
none decisive.

Though we took a vast number of prizes
from the French, yet they made themselves
masters of Minorca, as they did of Nevis and
St. Christopher, in the West Indies; and
Demerara and Issequibo soon shared the
same fate. Soon after, admiral Rodney had a
partial engagement with the count de Grasse,
who retired to Guadaloupe to refit; but not
long after the two fleets met, and a general
engagement commenced, which lasted twelve
hours, when four French ships were taken,
and one sunk; a fifth was taken, but blew
up. Admiral Hood captured four, and admiral Barrington two ships of war, and ten
sail under their convoy. The count de Grasse
was taken and brought to England; but most
of the prizes, with some of our own ships,
were lost in their passage.

The Spaniards took from us the Bahama
islands, and continued the siege of Gibraltar
with a vigorous perseverance; but all their
efforts were rendered ineffectual by the
bravery and conduct of general Elliot. He
again

again permitted them almost to complete their works, when he began such a heavy fire of carcasses, hot shot and shells, that several of their batteries were damaged, and some destroyed. The English also forced seven Spanish and two French ships of the line, with several smaller ones, to retreat. Soon after, another attack was made by ten floating batteries, built by the Spaniards at an enormous expence; but by an incessant fire of red-hot balls from the besieged, most of them were set in flames; when captain Curtis, with two English gun-boats, advanced, and prevented their receiving any assistance from the Spanish fleet. The humanity of captain Curtis saved 357 of the enemy. Great numbers, however, must have been killed and blown up. Fresh supplies were, soon after, thrown into Gibraltar by lord Howe, who had a partial engagement with the combined fleets, off the mouth of the Straits.

A complete change now took place in the ministry, at the head of which the marquis of Rockingham was placed; overtures were made for a general pacification; some indulgences were granted to Ireland; several useless places were abolished; and some fruitless attempts were made for a more equal representation in parliament. On the death of the marquis of Rockingham, lord Shelburne

P

(now

(now marquis of Lansdown) took the lead in administration, and several resignations followed. This year, the Royal George, of 100 guns, was unfortunately overset, when the brave admiral Kempenfelt, and near 600 other persons, were drowned in her.

In 1783, the provisional articles between England and America were made public. By these it appeared, that his Britannic Majesty acknowledged the independence of the United States of New Hampshire, Massachusetts Bay, Rhode Island and Providence Plantations, Connecticut, New York, New Jersey, Pennsylvania, Delaware, Maryland, Virginia, the Carolinas, and Georgia. He also relinquished all claims to the government of them, and consented to treat with those people as free and independent states, who, but a little time before, were despised as unpardonable rebels. Their boundaries were also settled, and they were allowed the liberty of fishing, and drying fish as usual. It was agreed, that the creditors on both sides should meet with no impediment in the prosecution of their claims. The restoration of confiscated property was also *recommended;* all prisoners were to be set at liberty; the English troops were to be immediately withdrawn from America; and a firm and perpetual peace was concluded between the contracting parties.

In our treaty with the French, after settling
the

the fisheries, the islands of St. Pierre, St. Lucia, Tobago, and Goree were surrendered to France, with the river Sehegal and its dependencies, and the forts St. Louis and others. The islands of Grenada, the Grenadines, St. Vincent, Dominica, St. Kitt's, Nevis, and Montserrat, were left to the English; the islands which the English had taken from the French in the East Indies were restored; and the prisoners on both sides were to be surrendered without ransom.

With the Dutch, our negociations were not so easily settled. However, after much deliberation, and several memorials, it was stipulated by treaty, that the king of Great Britain should restore Trincomalee, and all the possessions that had been taken during the war, to the Dutch; and that the States General should guarantee Negapatam, with its dependencies, to his Britannic majesty; and that mutual conquests were to be given up without compensation.

Our treaty with the Spaniards determined, that his Catholic majesty should maintain Minorca and West Florida, and to have East Florida ceded to him; and that Spain should surrender the island of Providence and the Bahamas to the English. All other conquests of territories were mutually to be restored without compensation.

At home, the preliminary articles of peace
P 2

were

were canvassed with great freedom in both houses of parliament.

Some important motions were carried against the ministry in the House of Commons; and after various and ineffectual struggles, the earl of Shelburne and his party resigned, and the duke of Portland was placed at the head of the new administration, while Mr. Fox took the lead in the lower house. Mr. Pitt, the son of the great earl of Chatham, made a motion for a parliamentary reform, which did not succeed. The next important event was a decision in the house of lords, by which bonds of resignation respecting church-livings were declared illegal by a decision of that house. This was followed by another unsuccessful attempt to bring on a reform. Parliament consented to a bill for the relief of the American loyalists; for ordering the establishment of the prince of Wales; and for granting pensions to lord Rodney and general Elliott, for their important services. Soon after, the parliament was prorogued, and the 6th of October was marked by the proclamation of peace.

Soon after the meeting of parliament, in November, Mr. Fox brought forward a bill, for the regulation of India, which was carried through the lower house by a great majority, but was rejected in the upper house. On the following night, Dec. 11, the ministry were
suddenly

suddenly dismissed, and Mr. Pitt was announced first lord of the treasury. This change was not expected to be permanent; and so strong was Mr. Fox's party in the House of Commons, that noblemen were at first afraid of accepting places of responsibility. These apprehensions were soon conquered; but still the minister found himself in a minority. Several addresses were presented by the opposition to his majesty, and all public business seemed to cease. The ministry, however, were determined, and refused to resign. Attempts were made to form a coalition, but they proved unsuccessful; and the parliament was dissolved on the 24th of March. The next parliament met on the 18th of May, 1784, when it was soon discovered, that there was a considerable majority on the side of the minister. When the election for Westminster, in which Mr. Fox complained of the illegal proceedings of the high-bailiff, was discussed, the minister carried almost every motion; notwithstanding which Mr. Fox at last triumphed, and sat as member for the city of Westminster. The minister brought forward his taxes, and his India bill, all which passed some of them without even a division. Laws were also made for the prevention of smuggling, the support of the public revenue, and for the restoration of the Scotch titles which had been forfeited in the rebellion. At length, after a long and busy session, the

parliament

parliament was prorogued on the 10th of August.

The year 1785 was also a period of political contention. Mr. Pitt presented to the house a string of propositions, tending to settle the commerce of England and Ireland on a mutual and equitable footing. They met with great opposition in both houses; and though they with difficulty passed, they were so increased and mutilated, as to retain hardly any thing of their original form. On being sent over to Ireland, they met with great opposition in that kingdom, and were soon thrown out with contempt, both countries considering them as destructive to their own interests.

In 1787, the French party fomented great disturbances in Holland, insinuating that the stadtholder sacrificed the interest of the republic to English politics; but the king of Prussia took so active a part in favour of the stadtholder, as totally frustrated the view of the French, who were in too distressed a situation to give the malcontents any assistance.

In this year also, Warren Hastings, esq. late governor of the English settlements in the East Indies, was accused of high crimes and misdemeanors during his government in the East. The matter was brought forward in the House of Commons by Mr. Burke, Mr. Sheridan, and some others, who impeached

Mr.

Mr. Hastings, and brought him to trial in the House of Lords.

About the same time some English merchants sent a vessel to Nootka, or King George's Sound, in the north-west part of America, to trade with the natives in furs, when the Spaniards seized the vessel, and treated the captain and his crew with great severity. This produced complaints from the British court to that of Spain; but our remonstrance being little attended to, both nations proceeded to make very powerful naval preparations; but the matter was at last patched up by a kind of treaty, which by the generality of people was considered as very vague and indeterminate.

This naval armament was hardly dismissed when a new object arose for collecting it together again. In the year 1788, the empress of Russia, who wished to obtain a port in the Black Sea, made very heavy claims on the Turks, and prevailed on the emperor of Germany to join in her views; but the war did no honour to the emperor, as the Turks cut some thousands of his troops to pieces, and many more perished by fatigue, want, and disease.

The empress of Russia, however, was more fortunate; she defeated the Turks in every battle, and took from them several places, particularly the forts Ockzacow and Ismael. These successes alarmed the British court, who

who fitted out a large fleet, in order to prevent Russia's obtaining the navigation of the Black Sea ; but the empress seemed to ridicule the preparations England was making, and insisted on maintaining the advantages she had acquired. Negociations commenced ; but the court of London, finding the empress was not to be intimidated, at last consented to disarm their navy, which had occasioned the nation an enormous expence, and leave the Russians in possession of their conquests. In or about the month of August, 1791, the preliminaries of peace were signed between the Russians and the Turks, by which the empress obtained the free navigation of the Black Sea, with the full possession of Ockzacow, and all its appendages, from the Neister to the Bog.

In 1788 the king of England was seized with a violent disorder, and continued ill a long time, with very little hopes of recovery.

In December, the Parliament met, but could not proceed to business, as they consisted only of two branches of the legislature, the third, the king, being incapable of acting. The prince of Wales was proposed as regent during his majesty's indisposition ; but the power with which he was to be invested occasioned very violent debates in both houses.

This contest continued till March 10, 1789, when his majesty sent a message to the house, to acquaint them with his sudden recovery, and his ability to attend to the public business of the nation.

In the month of July, one of the most unexpected revolutions took place in France that ever happened in the political hemisphere of Europe. The French king was divested of all his absolute authority, and reduced to one of the most limited monarchs in Europe. The Bastile, that den of slavery and cruelty, was so effectually demolished by the populace, as literally not to leave one stone upon another. The national assembly, who were chosen by the people, took from the king the power of making war and peace, and abolished all titles of peerages, it being their opinion, that no distinctions should be known, but such as arise from virtue, genius, and merit.

On the 14th of July, 1790, a solemn festival was held at Paris, when the French monarch made a formal surrender of the power which is dangerous in the hands of any single man. On the same day, in the Field of Mars, he took a solemn oath to abide by the new constitution, as prescribed by a decree of the national assembly. However, he soon afterwards endeavoured to make his escape to the German dominions, but he was stopped on the borders of Flanders, brought back to Paris, and closely guarded in one of the royal palaces. In the mean time the national

assembly

assembly drew up a new code of laws, and presented them to the king to sign, which he did on September 14, 1791, and by that means allayed the popular tumults.

Several matters of great importance were brought before parliament. In a committee of the house, appointed to hear and examine evidence on the slave trade, Mr. Wilberforce moved, that the chairman might be instructed to move for leave to bring in a bill to prevent the farther importation of African negroes into the British colonies. Although this question was supported by the great abilities of Mr. Francis, Mr. W. Smith, Mr. Fox, and even Mr. Pitt, yet it was lost in a minority of 75. However, this miscarriage gave birth to the plan of establishing a colony at Sierra Leona, on the African coast, from the success of which it was expected that the importance of the West India trade would in time be lessened. The Catholics, too, on their protesting against the universal supremacy of the pope, were released from certain disabilities and penalties to which persons of their persuasion were subject. Lastly, the constitution of Canada was settled by a bill which divided that province into Upper and Lower Canada, separated the government of these divisions, gave a council and house of assembly to each, ordered the taxes to be levied and disposed by the respective legislatures, and empowered those legislatures to

make

make new and alter former laws, as in their wisdom should seem fit.

An event of another kind, in which the nation has much cause to rejoice, must not be here omitted; the espousal of his royal highness the duke of York with the princess Frederica Charlotta Ulrica Catharina, daughter of the late king of Prussia; a lady of the most exalted virtue—visiting the humble cottage, succouring the laborious peasant, and alleviating distress in all its variety of shapes.

On the 16th of March, 1792, his majesty of Sweden, at a masquerade ball, was mortally wounded by a pistol fired at him by one of the masquers. Justice did not fail to overtake the perpetrator.

In the East Indies, Lord Cornwallis, having in a war with Tippoo Saib reduced him to extreme distress, concluded a peace upon his own terms, and received Tippoo's two sons as hostages for his fulfilment of them.

Mr. Fox introduced a bill for ascertaining the rights of juries in matters of libel, by the passing of which it was decided, contrary to the opinion of the law lords, that juries are judges both of the law and the fact.

The spirit of discussion, excited by the revolutionary proceedings in France, having produced various publications of seditious tendency, a royal proclamation was issued to suppress it, and prosecutions were instituted

against

against the authors of several books. On this occasion, his majesty received addresses of loyalty from both houses of parliament, as well as from the public bodies throughout the kingdom.

The minds of the people, however, were greatly agitated by the accounts daily received of measures pursued by the French revolutionists, which highly concerned the interests, and were of a nature to awaken the suspicion, not only of this, but also of the other surrounding governments. Some portion of disaffection is to be found in every country; there were appearances of no small mass of it in this, especially amongst the lower orders, who made no scruple of openly uttering expressions of sedition and anarchy.

A second proclamation, therefore, was issued, in which it was declared, that the evils before complained of had increased: that evil-disposed persons were acting in concert with others in foreign parts, in order to subvert the laws and constitution; and that a spirit of tumult and disorder, having lately manifested itself in acts of riot and insurrection, his majesty had forthwith resolved to embody a part of the national militia. This proclamation spread no inconsiderable alarm throughout the realm, and was followed by the adoption of very vigorous measures on the part of government. Indeed, the generality

rality of the nation were by no means back-
ward in seconding its endeavours for the public peace; on the contrary, they gave every
demonstration of attachment to the constitution. Associations were formed for opposing
the principles of " republicans and levellers;"
loyal addresses were presented, and writ-
ings continually dispersed against the French
and their abettors. In parliament, too, an
act passed to enable his majesty to force fo-
reigners out of the kingdom, and another
to prevent the exportation of corn into
France.

The French complained of these two measures loudly, as infractions of the commercial
treaty subsisting between the two nations,
not choosing to consider them as had recourse
to in consequence of their own recent offensive conduct. In particular, they had publicly resolved to extend their *fraternity* and
assistance to the revolting subjects of all mo-
narchial, or, as the convention chose to call
them, tyrannical governments; and they had
determined to open the navigation of the
Scheldt, notwithstanding they knew this
country was bound to oppose it. These
were points of which the British ministry
could not but demand the disavowal; but
this not being complied with to their satisfaction, M. Chauvelin, ambassador from the
late king, but not acknowledged in that light

from

from the republic, was ordered to quit the kingdom, by virtue of the alien act.

The 10th of August was rendered famous to the utmost verge of the politically intelligent world, as the epoch of the downfall of the ancient monarchy of France, by a furious attack made on the palace of the Thuilleries at Paris,. wherein the few who loyally maintained their stations in defence of the royal family, chiefly the Swiss-guards, were overcome and murdered, and the royal family forced to take refuge in the national assembly. The king was soon afterwards formally deposed, and imprisoned, with his family, in the Temple.

The 2d of September was rendered, if possible, still more notorious than the 10th of August, by a frantic mob's breaking open the prisons in Paris, and murdering such unhappy persons confined therein as had by their avowed, or imputed loyal sentiments exposed themselves to the effects of their malice. The innocent princess de Lamballe was one who fell under their infernal vengeance. Her head was carried about the streets upon a pole.

The world was awfully impressed, the beginning of the year 1793, by one of those events which are not often found in the annals of civilized nations, the putting a sovereign to death. Louis XVI. of France, after a trial which terminated in sentencing him to

lose

lose his life, was guillotined on the 21st of January.

Again in October, the public feelings were most sensibly affected by the trial of the queen of France on the 14th, and her execution on the 16th of that month.

On the 6th of November was also executed the duke of Orleans, cousin to the late king of France; but his conduct, when living, had left nothing in remembrance to cause any one to regret his death.

The famous countess du Barrè, formerly mistress of Louis XV. made another of the multitude of sufferers.

A declaration of war on the part of the French republic had taken place against the king of Great Britain, and the stadtholder of the United Provinces.

Great Britain, without making any formal declaration of war, soon entered into the active scenes of it, joining a confederacy formed between Germany and Prussia, and sending troops to the continent under the command of the duke of York. The combined armies defeated the French generals Valence, Miranda, and Dumourier, and took the cities of Valenciennes and Conde. The duke of York proceeded to attack Dunkirk, but this design he was compelled to abandon with loss.

Spain having also joined the coalition, a fleet of ships from that country, and an English

lish

lish fleet under lord Hood, proceeded to Toulon, which, by consent of the inhabitants, they took possession of in the name of Louis XVII. and garrisoned with eighteen thousand men of different nations. Not long afterwards, however, that city being powerfully attacked on the land side, and the allies being unable to maintain their station, set fire to the stores and shipping of the enemy which could not be carried off, and retired, with a considerable number of royalists.

In 1794 an alarm having been spread in the nation, from the apprehension of an invasion with which it was menaced by the French, great exertions were made by government to put the kingdom into a due state of defence, and military associations were lawfully organized in all parts for that purpose. These associations became very popular, and doubtless, from the readiness of young men to enter into them, had a sensible effect on the enemy, whose mighty preparations soon afterwards began to slacken, and at last were entirely dropped.

By virtue of warrants from the secretary of state, several seditious societies were suppressed, and their papers seized : these affording strong grounds to charge some leading and active men amongst them with high treason, they were accordingly apprehended and brought to the bar, but eventually acquitted.

quitted. Amongst them were Mr. Horne Tooke, Mr. Hardy, and Mr. Thelwall.

At this time the war on the continent proved very disastrous to the combined armies ; nevertheless the spirits of the English were superlatively elated by a glorious nava victory, obtained by the gallant veteran lord Howe, over a French fleet, which had ventured out of Brest harbour for the purpose of sheltering a convoy of expected mer-chantment. A partial action took place on the 28th of May ; but a general one ensued on the 1st of June. After very hard fighting on both sides, the French fleet was totally defeated, with the loss of six ships of the line taken and three sunk. From the crippled state of the English fleet, however, the merchantmen got safe into port. The French fleet consisted of twenty-six, the English of twenty-five ships of the line.

In the West-Indies, too, we were successful, taking Martinico, St. Lucie, and Guadaloupe ; and no less in the East, where the capture of Pondicherry, Chandinagore, and Mahie, added fresh lustre to the British arms.

After the evacuation of Toulon, lord Hood besieged and took the island of Corsica, the crown of which was afterwards presented to his majesty, who for some time governed the island by a viceroy ; but both that and the crown have been since relinquished.

Q 3

The

The innocent Madame Elizabeth, sister to the late king of France, was guillotined at Paris on the 10th of May ; and on the 28th of July, the tyranny of Robespierre met its deserved fate at Paris, by his being overthrown and guillotined, with twenty of his infamous adherents.

A dreadful fire broke out on the 24th of July, near Ratcliffe Cross, which could not be got under before 600 houses were consumed. The loss was computed at 1,000,000l. sterling.

A scandalous practice, called *Crimping*, which the exigency of the times had suffered to prevail to an alarming degree, occasioned many outrageous proceedings among the populace, during the month of August. Some regulations, however, were adopted by government, which soon allayed this ferment.

The old sentiments of reciprocal regard and affection between the British and American nations seemed to be revived by a treaty of amity and commerce, concluded the 19th of November.

In 1795, from the misfortunes which had attended the allied armies in the preceding campaign, and during the uncommonly severe winter which followed, and which afforded singular advantages to the French, not only the Austrian Netherlands, but the Dutch territories also, being over-run by them, the

stadtholder

stadtholder and his family were obliged to seek refuge in this country, and landed at Harwich the 21st of January. Hampton-court was assigned for their residence.

Our superiority at sea, however, continued to be maintained by another victory on that element, which was obtained by lord Bridport, close in with l'Orient; when, after an engagement of three hours, three French line of battle ships were captured, the Alexander, Formidable, and Tiger. Had there been a little more sea-room between the French fleet and their coast, no doubt the fruits would have been still more valuable.

There being from the present situation of affairs every reason to apprehend a rupture with the Dutch, an embargo was, on the 24th of January, laid upon the shipping and property of that nation, in the port of London, to the amount of 200,000l. sterling.

In April, the long protracted trial of Warren Hastings, esq. terminated in his acquittal, by almost all the peers who voted on the occasion.

A very interesting event marked this period—the marriage of his royal highness the prince of Wales with her serene highness the princess Caroline, daughter of the duke of Brunswick, which took place on the 8th of April.

Various disturbances broke out in the kingdom, amongst the poor, on account of the
dearness

dearness of bread ; a cause which never fails to create discontent. The price of a quartern loaf was then fifteen pence.

On the 26th of August, Trincomalee, a Dutch settlement in the East Indies, was added by capture to the British possessions in those parts.

Notwithstanding all the vigorous measures which had been put in force to stop the progress of sedition, and preserve the public peace, the political frenzy of the disaffected had increased to a very alarming degree. Not only were various assemblies holden in fields and other places, where the leaders harangued the multitude in the most inflammatory manner imaginable; but, as it was thought that matters were now sufficiently mature for commencing acts of violence, on the opening of parliament, the day before which care had been taken to hold one of these meetings, his majesty was most grossly insulted, and even his person endangered, in passing to the House of Lords. Stones and a variety of other things were thrown at his carriage ; and, whilst near Margaret-street, somewhat, supposed to be a bullet from the manner of its passage, perforated one of the windows, but happily without injuring his majesty, or any other person in the carriage. A reward of one thousand pounds was immediately offered by proclamation for the discovery of any person concerned in these

outrages ;

outrages, but without effect; the more fla-grant offenders not being detected, escaped their highly merited punishment: a journey-man printer convicted of having hissed and hooted the king, was the only person who suffered in any degree on this occasion, being sentenced to confinement during five years, and some other punishments.

It is not to be wondered at, that, under these pressing circumstances, two bills passed both houses of parliament, which would not have been approved of under others of less weight; one for the better security of his majesty's person, the other for the more ef-fectual prevention of seditious meetings and assemblies. These acts greatly strengthened and enlarged the power of magistrates, and they were accordingly required to exert them-selves to the utmost, by exercising the means they now possessed, in preventing those as-semblies of the people which were convened for the purpose of political declamation.

In December, for the first time this war, a royal message of a pacific nature was de-livered in both houses of parliament, purport-ing that the government of France having assumed somewhat of a regular form, his majesty was now ready to listen to any dis-position to negociate on the part of the ene-my; and to conclude a treaty of general peace whenever it could be effected on just and suitable terms for himself and his allies.

An

An overture was accordingly made on the part of his majesty, but so captiously, if not insolently, treated by the rulers in France, that his majesty could not with honour take farther steps towards the attainment of the desirable object in view.

In 1796, The seven United Provinces, being now become a republic upon the French model, and an ally of France, became also exposed to hostilities from this country, and in consequence lost several of their colonies and much of their shipping. Our arms were also turned against Spain, which had been constrained by France to withdraw from our alliance, and declare against us.

In the mean time the French, without the least colour or pretence of right, prosecuted a most successful campaign in Italy, under Bonaparte, a young man of extraordinary talents, whose character, from the various scenes and transactions in which he has since been engaged, may now be pretty accurately judged of.

On the 7th of January, her royal highness the princess of Wales was brought to bed of a daughter, which was afterwards christened Charlotta Augusta.

In the West Indies, the island of St. Lucia was taken by Sir Ralph Abercromby, on the 25th of May.——On the 16th of July, captain Trollope, in the Glatton, of 54 guus, acquired

quired great eclat by engaging and beating off a French squadron of eight ships, viz. one of 50, two of 36, three of 28, one of 18, and one of 12.—-The British navy also acquired fresh strength and laurels by admiral Elphinstone's capturing, on the 16th of August, a large Dutch fleet, under the command of admiral Lucas, near the Cape of Good Hope, without firing a gun. The Dutch spice islands also surrendered to the forces sent against them.

A memorable event took place in America, the 17th of August, by general Washington's resigning the presidency of that country. Mr. Adams was his successor.

On the 18th of October the Spaniards declared war against England; and the 17th of November was marked by the death of the empress of Russia, who was succeeded by the grand duke Paul Petrowitz.

The patriotism as well as opulence of this country were evinced to the world December 5, by a loan of 18,000,000l. being raised for government by voluntary subscriptions in 15 hours and 20 minutes.

Towards the end of this year, another attempt was made to negociate a peace, for which purpose lord Malmesbury was delegated to Paris; but, after a considerable length of time spent in fruitless discussion, he was informed that his proposals could not

be

be listened to, and that he must leave Paris in eight-and-forty hours.

In the beginning of the year 1797 it was found expedient to stop the payment in specie at the Bank.   However extraordinary this step, it created no great sensation of inquietude in the public mind, especially after an authentic account of its real state had, upon the fullest examinations, been announced: its notes passed as freely as ever: and for the better accommodation of the public, those of one pound value were now first issued.

On the 14th of February, a signal victory was obtained off Cape St. Vincent, by Sir John Jervis, commanding fifteen sail of the line, over the Spanish fleet of twenty-seven. After an engagement of five hours, in which the vast superiority of British naval tactics, skill, and bravery, was amply displayed, he captured two ships of 112 guns, one of 84, and one of 74.   As a reward for this eminent service, Sir John was created an earl, by the title of earl St. Vincent, in allusion to the scene of action.

But an unexpected cloud now cast an alarming gloom over our bright naval prospect.   A mutiny broke out among the seamen of the channel fleet, lying at Spithead: they deprived their officers of the command of the ships, and even threatened some of

them

them with the loss of their lives. On enquiring into the reason of this outrageous conduct, a variety of demands were made, the chief whereof was an increase of pay; which being considered by government as not altogether unreasonable, was complied with, to the re-establishment of order and discipline amongst them. Scarcely was this tumult appeased, when another broke out among some ships at Sheerness, which were joined by other ships, of which the refractory part of the crews had gotten the command. New and very extravagant demands being now made, and delegates chosen to conduct the mutiny, government determined to yield nothing more than was complied with on the former occasion at Portsmouth, and proceeded to take vigorous measures to reduce the mutineers to their duty. Upon their receiving intelligence of these intentions, dissentions soon began to arise amongst them, and after some time, they all ship by ship surrendered. Many of the ringleaders were hanged, the first of whom was Parker, whose case made much noise at the time; others suffered different punishments according to their different degrees of guilt, and the less criminal were indulged with a free pardon.

The stigma thus brought on the character of the British seamen, a great many of them had soon after an opportunity of wiping away; for, on the 14th of October, admiral Duncan,

 who

who had been waiting all the summer off the Texel for the Dutch fleet, had an opportunity of coming to an engagement, close to their own coast, and, after a most obstinate combat, captured no less than nine of their largest ships, and two admirals. For this great atchievement, the gallant admiral was raised to the peerage, with the dignity of viscount.

Three such transcendently glorious victories as we have recorded under Howe, Jarvis, and Duncan, were all followed by the appointment of a day of solemn and general thanksgiving to the Great Disposer of events for the same; and their majesties, together with the members of both Houses of Parliament, attended its celebration in St. Paul's cathedral.

A third negociation for peace was now set on foot at Lisle, but great obstacles presented themselves; and after the conferences had been protracted till September, lord Malmesbury finding it totally useless to continue them longer, returned to England.

The 17th of February, the island of Trinidad was taken, together with four ships of war in the bay; and on the 22d of the same month, fifteen hundred French ragamuffin troops having been put on shore at Fishguard, in South Wales, and abandoned by their countrymen, were all made prisoners.

An

An augmentation in the pay of the military forces of this kingdom took place the 14th of May; and on the 18th of the same month, the princess royal of England was married to the hereditary prince of Wirtemberg.

On the 28th of August, voilent riots ensued at Tranent, and other parts of Scotland, in consequence of the enforcement of the militia act.

A new gold coinage of 7s. pieces was issued at the Bank, the 2d of December, and declared current coin.

John Wilkes, esq. alderman and chamberlain, and once renowned patriot, died on the 26th of December.

On the 2d of April, 1798, Mr. Pitt made a proposal in the House of Commons, for the redemption of the land tax; and after the subject was debated both in and out of parliament till nothing remained to be said upon it, an act passed for the purpose, which received the royal assent by commission, the 21st of June.

For a long time past discontent had been rankling in the bosom of great numbers of the Irish, who, styling themselves " United Irishmen," had formed a very extensive conspiracy against the government. Numerous and shocking barbarities were committed upon those unhappy persons whom they conceived to be their enemies; but their opera-

tions

tions were chiefly confined at first to the night. However, they at length dared to appear in force, and committed acts of open violence and rebellion; insomuch, that on the 30th of March, the lord lieutenant (lord Camden) found it necessary to issue a proclamation, in which the most direct and positive orders were given to the officers commanding his majesty's forces, " to employ them with " the utmost vigor and decision for the im-" mediate suppression thereof, and also to " recover the arms which had been traitor-" ously forced from his majesty's peaceable " and loyal subjects, and to disarm the " rebels and all persons disaffected to his " majesty's government by the most sum-" mary and effectual measures." The loyal inhabitants were also required to aid and assist the military in carrying the proclamation into effect. General Abercromby was then at the head of the army in Ireland; and he caused general notice to be circulated throughout the kingdom of the orders contained in the above mentioned proclamation, and demanded a restitution and surrender of all the arms either taken or concealed, within ten days from the 3d of April, the persons so surrendering them being assured of suffering no kind of violence; but on the contrary, those who should withhold or conceal the said arms, would have the troops " quartered in large bodies, to live at free-

" quarters

" quarters among them," besides experienc-
ing other very severe measures which would
be resorted to, in order to enforce obedience.

These measures were attended with considerable success, but by no means sufficient to
prevent the growth of the conspiracy; for
on the 22d of May the lord lieutenant sent a
message to both houses of parliament, ac-
quainting them, that the magistrates of
Dublin had made application to him " to
" place the city under the provisions of the
" act passed in the 36th year of his majesty's
" reign;" which he had complied with :—
and farther, that the disaffected had been
daring enough " to form a plan for the pur-
" pose of possessing themselves, in the
" course of the present week, of the me-
" tropolis, of seizing the seat of govern-
" ment, and those in authority in the city."
His excellency hoped, however, to be able
to prevent the accomplishment of those outrageous designs.

Two days before this communication to
parliament, lord Edward Fitzgerald was
apprehended at the house of one Murphy, a
feather merchant, in Thomas Street. Thither Mr. Alderman Swan, Major Sirr, town-
major, and capt. Ryan, repaired in three
coaches as privately as possible. They
entered his room separately, by which means
he had the opportunity of doing much mis-
chief before he could be subdued. With a

 most

most destructive instrument of a new and
curious construction, he ran Mr. Swan
through the body above the shoulder blade,
and with one cut opened the belly of capt.
Ryan to such a degree that his bowels fell
out.   He was making another desperate
effort at major Sirr, when he received from
him a pistol shot in the shoulder, and was
forced to yield.   After examination at the
castle, he was conveyed to Newgate.

In the perturbed and dangerous state the
kingdom of Ireland now was, the British
government judged it prudent to set at the
head of it a military man of tried integrity
and abilities; and perhaps a fitter person
could not have been found than the marquis
Cornwallis, who was appointed lord lieutenant, and arrived at Dublin on the 20th of
June.   In the mean time, however, his predecessor, lord Camden, had so successfully
exerted himself, that the rebels were discom-
fited in all parts, and driven from their strong
holds, particularly from Vinegar Hill, where
they had assembled in great numbers.

The marquis Cornwallis seems to have
approved of the plan of operations adopted
by the military; they continued to pursue
it steadily and vigorously, and with their
accustomed success.   Nevertheless, on the
27th of June, the marquis published a proclamation, offering his majesty's pardon to
all such insurgents as should, within four-

teen

teen days, surrender themselves and their arms, and forsake their leaders who had seduced them.

What with the effect of the proclamation and the destruction of the sword and halter, it was calculated that 25,000 human beings had lost their lives, some of them of high consideration. The rebellion was now generally suppressed: armed parties at times made their appearance in different quarters, and kept the military employed in scouring the country; but none of sufficient consequence to create any serious alarm.

On the 22d of August, a secret committee of the house of commons made a report, in which were developed the rise, progress, and objects of the insurgents in the late rebellion. It took its origin in 1791. In 1796 there were 100,000 " United Irishmen," armed with pikes, in the province of Ulster alone; but, being disconcerted by the measures taken against them, they adopted the plan of corrupting the other provinces.

In the evening of the same day, three French frigates appeared in the bay of Killala, and landed about 700 men, who immediately took possession of the town of Killala, and made a small party of the prince of Wales's fencible regiment prisoners. They established their head quarters at the castle, which was the residence of the bishop. They demeaned themselves much better than might have

have been expected; nay, proved their protectors against the violence of the rebels:
and the bishop's capability of speaking
French was highly serviceable to both parties
on the occasion.

This small body lost no time in advancing
into the country, and on the 27th attacked
general Lake at Castlebar, before his forces
were collected, and compelled him to retire
with the loss of six pieces of cannon.

Encouraged by this success, the French
ventured to make farther progress; but
finding that general Lake had received considerable reinforcements, and that marquis
Cornwallis himself was advancing against
them with a large body of troops, they
thought it most advisable to make a retrograde
movement, which they continued to do,
varying their routes in order to avoid their
pursuers; till the 8th of September, when
they were overtaken by general Lake's column. An action forthwith commenced,
which, after half an hour's contest, terminated
in the surrender of the whole French corps,
together with the Irish rebels who had joined
them, but who were not very numerous.

One of the most brilliant exploits ever
atchieved took place on the 19th of May;
the destruction of the Grand Bruges canal, by a handful of men (about 1300,)
under the command of general Coote. Having been landed, after a dangerous navigation

tion over sands in the night, conducted by capt. Popham himself, who had the command of the ships, immediately marched five miles up the country to the sluice gates of Bruges, totally destroyed the canal, by blowing up the works, and burnt several gun-boats and a number of transports. The information and instructions received had been so correct, and the execution so masterly, that in less than six hours the whole business was completed, and the men drawn up on the beach ready to be reimbarked. But most unfortunately this was prevented by a high surf in consequence of a change of wind, nor did it abate in the course of fourteen hours, by which time the enemy had collected a numerous body of troops, who attacked and compelled this little army to surrender. " Four hours moderate wea-
" ther," said an officer on the expedition,
" would have rendered this the most glo-
" rious, the most brilliant enterprize ever
" undertaken by this country; the want of
" it has thrown a gloom over success, and
" robbed us of our laurels !"

Report had made it well known throughout Europe, that great preparations were making by the French at Toulon, for an expedition of more than common magnitude and importance, and that it was to be conducted by the celebrated Bonaparte; but its destination was involved in impenetrable secrecy.

cresy. The British commanders in the Mediterranean were not wanting in their attention to the motions of the fleet, on board which it was preparing, hoping to intercept it on its putting to sea. It escaped all their vigilance, however, and Malta was captured almost before the course it had taken was known. From thence it steered towards Alexandria, in Egypt, and anchoring off Rosetta, situated at one of the mouths of the Nile, debarked unmolested the forces it had carried. Admiral Nelson, who was the person appointed to look after it, employed every means in his power to obtain a knowledge of its situation : but it happened, nevertheless, that he did not get a sight of it, for a considerable time. At length, however, on the 1st of August, he found them moored, in a strong line, across the bay of Aboukir, in a position which the French admiral thought to be perfectly secure. Admiral Nelson ordered an immediate attack, and by dexterously sending a part of his ships, (one of which grounded in the attempt) between the enemy's fleet and the shore, attacked it on both sides at once, ship after ship, in succession. A complete victory was the consequence ; after a most dreadful conflict, nine ships of the line were taken, and two burnt, one of which was L'Orient, the French admiral's, who was killed in the engagement. Only two ships of the line escaped of the whole

whole fleet. For this most glorious service, admiral Nelson was rewarded by an advancement to the peerage, with the title of Baron Nelson of the Nile, and a pension of 2,000l. per annum.

On the 3d of September war was declared at Constantinople against France.

A general thanksgiving for the successes obtained by his majesty's arms at sea, and in particular for the victory of the Nile, was appointed to be observed on the 29th of November.

On the 3d of December Mr. Pitt proposed a tax on all persons having incomes of and above 60l. per annum. The avowed principle of it was, the necessity of raising within the year a large proportion of supplies. A bill for the purpose was brought in, and violent was the opposition it met with; but with some modifications it at length passed through both Houses of Parliament, and received the royal assent by commission.

On the 22d of January, 1799, the measure or uniting the kingdoms of Great Britain and Ireland was proposed to the British parliament by a message from the king, in which his majesty expresses his firm persuasion, " that " the unremitting industry with which our " enemies persevere in their avowed design " of effecting the separation of Ireland from " this kingdom, cannot fail to engage the par- " ticular attention of parliament; and his ma-
" jesty

" jesty recommends it to both houses, to
" consider of the most effectual means of
" counteracting and finally defeating, this
" design, &c. &c."

The same measure was proposed on the
same day, by his excellency the lord-lieute-
nant, to the Irish parliament. In both parliaments the greatest opposition was made
to it, on the question for the address; but
with very different results. It was carried in
both houses of the British without a division;
it was also carried in the Irish House of
Lords by a majority of 32; but negatived in
the Commons by a majority of five. The
measure was therefore rejected in Ireland for
that Session. But, in England, Mr. Pitt followed up its success, in spite of the most determined opposition, till he had obtained the
passing through both houses a number of resolutions, explaining the nature, extent,
terms, &c. of his scheme, in order that the
Irish might take them into consideration in
their calm hours; after which, possibly they
might find themselves inclined to think more
favorably of and adopt them.

A fresh war having broke out in the East
Indies, in consequence of the perfidious and
treacherous conduct of Tippoo Sultan, lieutenant-general Harris, at the head of an army collected on the occasion, on the 4th of
May attacked and captured Seringapatam,
his capital. The sultan himself was slain

in

in the conflict; immense treasures were found in his palace; and the acquisition of a great extent of country, the delivery of the British possessions in India from the peril of foreign invasion, and their security and ease were the consequences of this victory.

Vast preparations had long been making for a grand expedition against Holland, and on the 7th of August the first division of troops began to embark at Ramsgate, Deal, Margate, &c. under the command of sir Ralph Abercromby. On the 13th the fleet sailed, and landed the troops on the 27th on the sands near the Helder point, and after a battle which lasted the whole day, defeated the Dutch and French, who abandoned in the night all the batteries of the Helder Point. Hereupon general Abercromby proceeded farther into the country, taking due care, however, to secure himself by fortifications and intrenchments; and on the 10th of the month the Dutch and French armies attacked the British, but were defeated at Schagenburg, with the loss of 1000 men, besides prisoners. The British lost about 200.

A second and a third division of British troops had sailed for Holland, the last of which, with a corps of Russians, arrived at the Helder on the 15th: the Duke of York had arrived there the day before. The whole effective force under his command was estimated to amount to 60,000 men.

On the 19th, the British and Russians, under the command of the Duke of York, attacked in three columns the Dutch and French armies, and got possession of Horne in Dyke and of Alkmaar, but the Russian column being defeated, the whole army returned to its former position. The British lost 1000 in killed, wounded, and prisoners ; the Russians 2000. On the 3d of October, the Duke of York attacked and drove the French and Dutch army from all their positions before Alkmaar, which opened its gates to the British the next morning. The British lost in killed, wounded, and missing, 1332, the Russians 593. On the 6th, the duke of York again attacked the enemy between Bever Wyke and Wyck-up-zee, and after a severe battle, compelled them to retire from the field. The British took 500 prisoners, but had 92 officers and men killed, 725 wounded, and 613 missing ; the Russians 382 killed or prisoners, and 735 wounded. The duke of York having learnt that the enemy had been reinforced with 6000 men, held a council of war, in which it was deemed necessary to withdraw the troops from Holland, to abandon Alkmaar, and retire to the position first occupied by general Abercromby, on the canal of Zype. On the 8th his royal highness concluded a convention with the French general Brune, by which it was agreed that the British

British army should have to the 30th of November to evacuate Holland, on condition of returning 8000 French and Dutch prisoners, and not damaging the country or works in their possession at the Helder. In consequence of this convention, the army prepared to return to England; the duke of York arrived in town the 4th of November, and by the 20th the Helder was finally evacuated, the whole of the British and Russian army having been re-embarked.

The command of the naval operations in this expedition was committed to admiral Mitchell, who, after the success of the troops at Helder, followed the flying Dutch fleet, and on the 28th and 30th took the whole of them, consisting of one of 74 guns, four of 68, one of 60, three of 54, six of 44, one of 32, six of 24, and one of 16. On the 21st of September he also captured Enkhuysen, and other towns on the Zuyder sea.

The question of the union between Great Britain and Ireland was revived in January 1800, and, notwithstanding the vigorous exertions of its opponents, its importance and utility were so powerfully insisted on by his majesty's ministers, that it was at length ratified by the parliaments of both kingdoms, and passed into a law, by royal assent, on the second of July.

In the month of February, two acts of considerable importance were passed, the one

for

for a suspension of the habeas corpus act, and the other for preventing mutiny and sedition. The legislature also prudently turned its attention toward the enormous price of provisions, which had resulted partly from the waste of war, and partly from a scanty harvest; and several laudable institutions were made for the relief of the poor in that distressing exigency: but our confined limits preclude the possibility of descending to particulars.

On the 11th of March, a society under the patronage of his majesty, and under the title of " The royal institution of Great Britain," commenced its first sittings, in order to direct the public attention to the arts, by an establishment for diffusing the knowledge of useful mechanical inventions and improvements.

On the 15th of May, while his majesty was attending some field exercises in Hyde Park, a ball cartridge was fired from one of the soldiers, which wounded Mr. Ongley, a clerk in the allotment part of the navy office, who was standing at a small distance from the king: and in the evening of the same day, a man named Hadfield discharged a pistol at our gracious sovereign, in Drury-lane theatre. This action, however, was productive of no misfortune, and the perpetrator was found, on examination, to be afflicted with a mental derangement.

The

The temporary consternation occasioned by these circumstances, was followed by several brilliant proofs of public loyalty; and the celebration of his majesty's birth-day, on the 4th of June, commenced with one of the grandest sights ever exhibited in Hyde Park. All the volunteer corps in London and its immediate vicinage assembled to the amount of 12,000, before eight o'clock, and gave the highest gratification to his majesty by their loyalty, decorum, and evolutions.

On the second of July his majesty went in state to the House of Peers, in order to give his assent to the union bill; on the 12th of the same month, the first stone of a new wet dock, near the Isle of Dogs, was laid with great solemnity, in the presence of several persons of distinction; and on the 29th his majesty closed the session of parliament by a speech from the throne.

Soon after the prorogation of parliament, the affluent inhabitants of London began to entertain serious apprehensions from the discontent of the lower orders; and their fears were partly realized by a disturbance in the prison of Cold Bath Fields, and by some riotous proceedings in the metropolis, and in various parts of the country: but government took effectual precautions for the preservation of order, and the rash attempts of the

unprincipled

unprincipled and disaffected, were happily rendered abortive.

During these transactions at home a squadron under Sir Edward Pellew destroyed the forts on the south-west of the peninsula of Quiberon; captured six brigs, sloops, and gun-boats; and intercepted the supplies which had been destined for the use of the French fleet off Brest. Sir Charles Hamilton also took possession of the Isle of Goree, on the coast of Africa; and a fleet under the command of Sir John Borlase Warren gained some advantages over the Spaniards at Ferrol.

On the fifteenth of September the island of Malta surrendered to the British troops, after a blockade of two years; and about the same time, Curaçao an island situated near the continent of South America, was surrendered by the Dutch to the English. On the 5th of October, the British fleet from the Mediterranean appeared before Cadiz; but, as the place was then infected by an epidemic disease, and the strength of the works was found to be very great, the armament was withdrawn.

In consequence of various petitions from the city of London, and other parts of England, the parliament was convened on the 11th of November, and an address of thanks was moved for his majesty's gracious speech on that occasion.

After

After several parliamentary debates and proceedings, relative to the dearth of provisions, the evacuation of Egypt, and the dismissal of his majesty's ministers, the king gave his sanction, on the 31st of December, to such bills as were deemed necessary to be passed; and (as the first day of the new year was to usher in a new form and title of government) the chancellor was ordered to read a proclamation, which declared that the individuals who composed the present parliament should be the members, on the part of Britain, of the parliament of the united kingdom of Great Britain and Ireland, and that the imperial parliament should be assembled on the 22d day of the ensuing century.

On the first of January, 1801, a proclamation was issued out concerning the royal style and titles, belonging to the imperial crown of Great Britain and Ireland, and also the ensigns, flags, banners, and armorial bearings. The royal style and title were to be " George the third, by the grace of God, of the united kingdom of Great Britain and Ireland, king, defender of the faith." The arms of the united kingdom were to be quarterly: first and fourth England; second Scotland; third Ireland. There was also to be borne with these, on an escutcheon of pretence, the arms of his majesty's German dominions ensigned with the electoral bonnet

net.   The quartering of the royal standard was to be the same with that of the arms of the united kingdom : and the union flag to be azure, bearing the crosses of St. George, St. Andrew, and St. Patrick.   Some orders were, likewise, issued out respecting the ensigns to be borne by merchant ships belonging to his majesty's subjects ; and a new great seal was made in conformity with the alterations which had taken place in the royal arms and titles.

The imperial parliament was opened, by commission, on the 22d of January, 1801, and on the second of the following month, his majesty went in state to the House of Peers, and made a speech, in which he adverted to the transactions of the last years ; expressed his satisfaction at the legislative union of the two kingdoms ; and avowed his intention of putting a termination to the war, as soon as that step could be taken with honour and security.   An address was immediately moved by the duke of Montrose, and, after several warm debates, presented to his majesty.

In the beginning of February, the situation of England might be said to have become truly critical, being literally encompassed with difficulties and dangers.   Repeated efforts to circumscribe the power of France had been rendered ineffectual ; the southern and western nations of Europe were

either

either detached from, or rendered hostile to the interests of our country; the ports of the Weser, Elbe, and Baltic, were unfortunately shut against us, while we expected a supply of grain from thence; and the indisposition of our gracious sovereign rendered it impossible for retiring ministers to deliver up the badges of their office.

In this posture of affairs Mr. Pitt determined to resign his offices of first lord of the treasury, and chancellor of the exchequer; and the resignation of that gentleman was followed by those of Mr. Dundas, earl Spencer, lord Grenville, and Mr. Windham. Various debates arose in the House of Commons in consequence of this circumstance; but, as our limits preclude the possibility of detailing them, it is only requisite to add, that Mr. Addington, (late speaker of the House) succeeded Mr. Pitt as chancellor of the exchequer; and an entire change took place in the administration.

On the 20th of March, the Invincible of 94 guns, captain Rennie, was unfortunately lost by running aground on the Norfolk coast; and upwards of four hundred persons perished, among whom were the captain and most of the officers. The 25th of the same month was marked by the death of Paul I. emperor of all the Russias, &c. who appears to have disgusted all ranks of his subjects, and is said to have been taken off by by violence, though his dissolution was publicly ascribed to an apoplexy.

In the morning of April 2d, lord Nelson engaged the Danish fleet, (consisting of six sail of the line, eleven floating batteries, and one bomb ship, besides several schooner gun-vessels near Copenhagen, and gained a decisive victory, after an obstinate and bloody conflict of four hours. In consequence of this circumstance, the thanks of the Commons were unanimously voted to admiral Sir Hyde Parker, vice admiral lord Nelson, rear admiral Graves, and colonel Stewart, for their bravery and gallant conduct. Monuments were also ordered to be erected, at the public expence, to the memory of captain James Robert Mosse, and captain Edward Riou, who fell gloriously in the discharge of their duty ; and a liberal pension was conferred, by the king, on captain Sir Thomas B. Thompson.

On the accession of Alexander to the imperial throne of Russia, harmony was re-established between the courts of London and Petersburgh ; and the termination of hostilities between Denmark and Great Britain was attended with such affecting circumstances as might be naturally expected in a reconciliation of friends.

Whilst the British arms were crowned with abundant success in various undertakings, the parliament passed several bills of a beneficial nature, particularly those for bounties on the importation of grain ; improvement of commons and waste lands ; repeal of the brown bread act ; relief of insolvent debtors ; and for preventing ,the arrest of aliens in Great Britain for debts contracted in France previously to the revolution. We must also observe that his majesty graciously conferred the dignity of a barony of Great Britain on the relict of sir Ralph Abercromby, who terminated a life of gallant service at Aboukir, and to whom a monument was justly decreed at the public expence.

On the 19th of June, the first stone of the Royal Military Asylum at Chelsea was laid, in presence of the duke of York, the secretary at war, lord Harrington, &c. and several medals, commemorative of our naval and military achievements were deposited under it.

About this time the naval strength of England was so great, that she had fleets in the Indian ocean, in the Red sea, at the mouth of the Nile, in the Mediterranean, in the Baltic, and in the West Indies : besides a channel fleet, detached cruizers and convoy ships in every direction ; and a flotilla of vessels which, under the command of lord Nelson, protected the British shores, and gave frequent causes of alarm to those of France. Of the various engagements which happened in the course of the summer, it is only necessary to say, that they generally reflected the

highest

highest honor on the cause and arms of the British empire.

England having been, for some time, threatened with an invasion by means of flat-bottomed boats; it was deemed expedient to turn the tide of war from defensive to offensive, and, after mature deliberation, it was determined that lord Nelson, with a flotilla of gun-boats, and other armed vessels, should carry the terrors of war to the enemy's shore.

On the 30th of July lord Nelson displayed his flag on board the Leyden, of 68 guns, at Deal, and took the command of an armament which had excited universal curiosity and attention, as being destined for a secret expedition. On the 1st of August the gallant commander stood over to the coast of France, and avowed his intention of making an attack upon Boulogne, where the enemy had been assembling their small craft, as was reported, for the purpose of a descent upon this country.

After reconnoitring the fortifications, and making other necessary arrangements, his lordship commenced the attack at day-break on the 4th instant, and a heavy firing ensued, by which six of the French vessels were so much damaged, that they were towed from the scene of action. It was the British admiral's intention to have sent, at the approach of night, three bombs close upon the enemy,

enemy, each bomb followed by ten boats; but a sudden change of the wind precluded the execution of this scheme, and the English vessels were obliged to haul off, after convincing the French, that they should not come out of their harbours with impunity.

Having received a considerable reinforcement from the Downs, and made a feint of sailing towards Flushing, or some other port on the Dutch coast, lord Nelson resolved to attempt the destruction or capture of the whole flotilla, amounting to twenty-five armed vessels, which were moored in the front of Boulogne. Accordingly on the evening of the 15th our vessels formed in four divisions to storm the adverse line of brigs, boats, and luggers, which were fastened to each other by means of strong iron chains, and defended by land batteries, as well as by musketry from the shore. Each of the English divisions had a proportionate number of vessels to attack; the first beginning to the eastward and proceeding in order to the westward. The boats put off from the Medusa at half past eleven at night, and a vigorous attempt was made to board a large brig, that was distinguished by the commodore's pennant; but the gallant exertions of the assailants were completely baffled by some strong netting that was braced to the lower yard, and by an instantaneous discharge of guns from about two hundred soldiers. By this acci-

T

dent

dent captain Parker was dreadfully wounded; his companions were all killed or disabled, and his boat hung alongside; in which situation it would have certainly been taken by the enemy, had not the honourable Mr. Cathcart taken it in tow, and carried it off.

Captain Williams led on his subdivision with extraordinary bravery, and made himself master of one lugger, notwithstanding most of his boat's crew were killed in the dreadful contest. Captains Conn, Jones, and Cotgrave, also exhibited the utmost firmness and resolution in their respective attacks: but the British troops were assailed by such volleys of musketry and grape shot, both from gun-boats and from the shore, and their attempts were so effectually foiled by the boarding netting, projecting spikes, and extended chains, that our gallant admiral was at length compelled to abandon his enterprize, with the loss of 172 men. The loss of the French is not accurately known, though it must have been very considerable. The admiral, Latouche Treville, acknowledged that our sailors and marines boarded his vessels with the utmost intrepidity, and described the deplorable spectacle that was presented on board their vessels after the action; the decks literally strewed with dead and dying, and mutilated limbs every where discovered, after the ensanguined corses were thrown into the sea.

These

These tremendous engagements in which
the discharge of so much artillery seemed to
shake both heaven and earth, were distinctly
heard on both sides the channel; and the first
during the 3d of August, was witnessed by
thousands of spectators, who covered the
hills of Boulogne and the cliffs of Dover.
This was perhaps the first spectacle of so
important a nature that was ever seen from
the shores of both countries.

On his arrival at Deal, lord Nelson exerted
himself in a very laudable manner, for the relief of the brave combatants, who had suffered severely in this unfortunate expedition.
His time was chiefly occupied in visiting the
wounded in the hospital, and his cordial sym-
pathy afforded a sensible consolation to most
of the sufferers. On asking one man how he
was, and hearing that he had lost an arm,
he told him not to regard it: for that he
himself had lost one also, and might soon lose
a leg; but that they could never be lost in a
better cause than that of defending his country. This observation produced the desired
effect; and many of the mangled veterans
exclaimed, in the enthusiasm of loyalty, that
they only regretted their wounds as they prevented them from accompanying so brave a
commander in another expedition.

The failure of his most brilliant projects in
Egypt, the sudden death of Paul 1. the dissolution of the northern confederacy, the un-

                         abated

abated vigor of the British government, and several concurring circumstances, now induced the Corsican consul to listen to pacific proposals. Preliminaries of peace were accordingly signed at Lord Hawkesbury's office on the first of October, and the ratification was brought to London on the 12th by M. Lauriston.

On the 29th of March, 1802, Mr. Moore (assistant secretary to Marquis Cornwallis) arrived in London with the definitive treaty, which had been signed at Amiens, on the 27th, by the plenipotentiary of his Britannic majesty, and by the plenipotentiaries of France, Spain, and the Batavian republic; and on the 29th of April, the proclamation of peace was performed at the usual places in London and Westminster.

The blessings of peace, however, were of short duration, owing to the perfidy and unbounded ambition of the French government; which imposed the most severe restrictions upon British commerce, and refused to restore some vessels captured in India after the signature of the preliminaries. At the same time the avies of Spain and Holland were held at the disposal of the first Consul; numerous persons were landed in different parts of Great Britain and Ireland under the name of commercial commissioners, but who were in reality military officers authorised to procure

cure surveys of certain places; and the report of Colonel Sebastian' mission to Egypt
contained the most malignant calumnies
against the British officers who commanded
in that quarter.

Some official papers presented to the British ministry, arraigning the liberty of the
press in England, and demanding that the
French princes, and other emigrants, should
be dismissed from the protection of his Britannic majesty, afforded just ground for a
suspicion that Bonaparte wished to interfere
and gain an ascendancy in our domestic con-
cerns, as he had previously done with respect to Holland, Spain, and other countries. And the annexation to France of the
territories of Piedmont, Parma, Placentia,
and the isle of Elba; together with the sub-
jugation of the Swiss Cantons, in direct
violation of the treaty of Luneville, exhibited
in striking colours the insatiable rapacity of
the French government.

Under these circumstances, the possession
of Malta became a subject of contention, and
a peremptory demand was made for its immediate evacuation, while the British ministry were insolently told, in an official do-
cument, that their country was unable to con-
tend *single handed* with France.

At this crisis, very considerable preparations were made in the ports of France and
Holland, which excited the attention of the

English ministry, and induced his majesty, on the 8th of March, 1803, to make a communication on the subject to both Houses of Parliament; and two days afterwards, a second message imported the necessity of calling out and embodying the militia, or such part thereof as his majesty might think proper for the defence and safety of his dominions.

A long and protracted correspondence had been carried on between the courts of Paris and London relative to the dispute respecting Malta, the emigrant princes, &c. But after much time had been exhausted, and an interview had taken place between Lord Whitworth and the Chief Consul, in which the latter displayed a surprising neglect of dignity and propriety, the British ambassador set out on his return; and on the 18th of May, Government published a declaration of their causes of complaint against France; which was soon followed by the issuing of letters of marque and reprisal.

Such was the general abhorrence of the French perfidy, and such the contempt of their threatened invasion, that, instead of repining at the short interval of peace, and the unfortunate necessity for a recommencement of hostilities, the heroism of the English nation seconded the vigour of Government so effectually, that our naval force was soon found to be double in number and spirit to

what

what we could boast at the beginning of any former war. The embodying of the militia was followed by the act for raising an army of reserve, which, in the course of a few months, added thirty thousand men to the regular force of the country; and an act enabling his Majesty to raise a *levy en masse*, was rendered unnecessary by the spontaneous zeal and loyalty of the people. Volunteer associations were formed in all parts of the country; ample subscriptions were raised in many of the principal towns; and, in short, the British public seemed to glory in the idea of offering their persons and property in defence of their enviable constitution: so that when our enemy thought to have snared the lion sleeping in his den, he found him prepared for battle, and ready to spring upon his prey.

On the opposite side of the channel, immense preparations were made, particularly at Boulogne, the harbour of which was strongly fortified. An army of three hundred thousand men was also marched to the coast, and vessels of a particular description were constructed in all the ports and navigable rivers of France and the Netherlands.

Finding, however, that England enjoyed the most perfect unanimity, and that her fleets and armies were too formidable to admit any hope of success in the projected invasion,

invasion, the French government exhausted its rage in empty menaces, and acts of perfidy and violence scarcely equalled in the darkest ages of society. At the very commencement of hostilities, a number of English travellers and others were inhospitably seized and committed to custody as prisoners of war; and towards the end of May, General Mortier was sent to seize the electorate of Hanover, thus violating the neutrality of the German empire, and acting diametrically opposite to the French republicans themselves, who a few years before, had concluded a separate peace with the elector of Hanover, while, as king of Great Britain, he continued at war with their country.—Notwithstanding the palpable inconsistency of this conduct, the French minister Talleyrand had the insolence to demand from his Britannic majesty the ratification of the treaty concluded between Mortier and the regency of Hanover: and it soon afterward appeared that an overture equally insolent had been made to Louis XVIII. at Warsaw, for the resignation of his right to the crown of France, for which he should receive indemnities and a splendid establishment from Bonaparte!

We must now look back to the beginning of the year, when an event occurred which served to develope the disposition of the enemy, even during the peace, but which

could

could not have been related before, without breaking the thread of our narration relative to the speedy renewal of hostilities:

Among the most active of the disaffected party in England, who held a secret correspondence with the French government, was Colonel Despard, a gentleman who had in his military career performed some brilliant exploits, and had been regarded as a meritorious officer, but who, having been disappointed in his expectations, and afterward contaminated by the principles of the French revolutionists, was at length induced to enter into the most treasonable designs against his king and constitution.

The active operations of this unfortunate man and his fellow conspirators commenced as early as the spring of 1802, when they administered an oath to every person admitted a member of their association, and exerted themselves to gain proselytes among the lowest and most profligate of the soldiery, who, in case of a revolution, were to be invested with high military rank. Their principal object was to murder the king as he returned from parliament at the opening of the session; while other parties were to seize the Tower and the Bank, to destroy the telegraph, and stop the mail coaches, which was to be a signal to the disaffected in the country to march to their assistance. Plausible, however, as this scheme was in speculation,

speculation, the number of the conspirators did not afford any hope of success; and after Government had prudently permitted the plot to ripen, so as to develope completely the designs of the conspirators, they were arrested at the Oakley Arms in South Lambeth, and committed to prison.

On the 7th of February, Colonel Despard was brought up for trial before a special commission at the New Session-House, Southwark; and after an eloquent defence, by his counsel, and honourable testimonies to his former conduct in the army, by Lord Nelson, Sir Alured Clark and Sir Evan Nepean, he was found guilty.—Two days afterwards, the court proceeded to the trial of twelve other of the conspirators, nine of whom were fully convicted. Three of these received his majesty's pardon, and the remaining six, with their unhappy leader, were executed on the 21st of the same month.

Such was the termination of this daring conspiracy; but Ireland had unfortunately afforded a fairer field for the emissaries of insurrection; and Mr. Emmett, who had recently returned from the continent, carried on his machinations with such effect, that he actually formed a depot of arms in an alley in Thomas-street, Dublin, and caused a large manufacture of pikes to be secretly carried on; while the other leading conspirators

pressed

pressed both men and horses into their service, and drew up a proclamation, purporting to be issued by the provisional government of Ireland.

Various rumors had been circulated, for some days, concerning an intended rising of the people; but the reports were so contradictory, that no reliance could be placed on them; and the only precaution taken, was that of doubling the patroles in particular stations. On the 23d of July, however, about nine o'clock in the evening, the appointed signal of rebellion was given by the firing of rockets; and Emmett, Quigley, Dowdall and Stafford, the four chief conspirators, rushed out of the depot at the head of their deluded followers, and took their station in Thomas-street, where the insurgents soon increased from fifty to five hundred. Groups of pikemen and other rebels were dispersed in various parts, while weapons were liberally dispersed among the mob, and the scene became truly tremendous.

During the height of the insurrection, Lord Kilwarden, lord chief justice of the king's bench, arrived from his country house accompanied by his daughter, Miss Wolfe, and his nephew, a young clergyman. His lordship and his nephew were immediately dragged from their carriage, and pierced with innumerable wounds, while

while Miss Wolfe escaped on foot, and fled to the Castle to relate the dreadful catastrophe.—Colonel Brown, a gentleman greatly repected, was another victim of the brutal multitude; and every casual passenger who escaped assassination, was compelled to join the insurgents.

After some time, however, Mr. Wilson, a police magistrate at the head of only eleven men, approached the scene of insurrection, and though surrounded by nearly three hundred pikemen, he firmly commanded them to lay down their arms; and after receiving a wound from one of the rebels, he and his men fired upon them, and threw them into confusion, though he was afterwards compelled to retreat. Lieutenant Brady, of the 21st fusileers, now advanced to the attack at the head of forty men, who being judiciously divided in smaller parties, kept up so well directed a fire, that the insurgents began to flee. Lieutenant Coltman soon arrived with about twenty-eight men, to assist the royalists; and the military pouring in from all quarters, the rebels were routed with great slaughter; and before twelve o'clock, the insurrection was completely quelled. Never was a rebellion crushed with greater facility or more general satisfaction. The subsequent proceedings against offenders were all constitutional, and the victims comparatively few, as Government proceeded with the

tardiness

tardiness of humanity and not with the rapidity of revenge.

From the nature of the contest, it might naturally be expected that the war at home should be, for the first year, chiefly defensive and preparatory. England, however, not only kept her haughty enemy at bay, and disconcerted all his projects, but abroad her arms were as successful as could have been hoped. On the 22d of June, the island of St. Lucia was taken by General Grinfield and Commodore Hood; and on the 30th, Tobago was surrendered to them by capitulation. The same meritorious commanders reduced the Dutch Islands of Demerara and Essequibo on the 19th of September; and on the 24th, the settlement of Berbice surrendered to his Britannic majesty's arms.

The calamities which the French endured at St. Domingo were dreadful in the extreme; and after the most obstinate resistance, General Rochambeau was obliged to elude the vengeance of the revolted negroes by surrendering to the English, with the whole army of the Cape, two frigates, and some other vessels which lay in the harbour.

In Europe, as we have already hinted, few offensive operations could be undertaken by the English. On the 14th of September, however, Sir James Saumarez made an attack on the port of Granville, where he
u demolished

demolished the pier, and destroyed many of
the vessels intended for the invasion of
England. On the same day, the town and
fort of Dieppe were bombarded by Captain
Owen; and several of the Dutch ports were
severely bombarded on the 28th, when many
of their vessels were destroyed.

The month of May, 1804, was marked by
a change of the British ministry; Mr. Addington having resigned, and Mr. Pitt being
appointed to resume his former office, together with the power of forming a new administration. Many reports had been circulated respecting a coalition between Mr.
Pitt, Mr. Fox, lord Grenville, &c. but the
result proved otherwise; and the reinstated
minister met with a most vigorous opposition from the minority. The additional
force bill, the corn bill, and several others
which he introduced into parliament, were
opposed in the most strenuous manner: but
all of them were passed by a considerable
majority.

On the 2d of July, a bill was passed, em-
powering the directors of the Bank of England to issue dollars as five shilling tokens,
after being stamped with suitable impressions,
at Mr. Bolton's mint in Birmingham.

On the 6th of August, intelligence was
received of an occurrence, which, being of
the highest national importance, and re-
flecting the most brilliant honor on the
British

British character, may probably be acceptable to our readers :—

Captain Nathaniel Dance had been dispatched from Canton on the 31st of January, in the Earl Camden East Indiaman, having under his care, as senior commander, a fleet of twenty-six ships. After a tedious passage down the river, he passed Macao Roads on the night of the 5th of February; and on the 14th, a signal was made for seeing five strange sail to the S. W. which were soon discovered to be an enemy's squadron, consisting of a line of battle ship, two frigates, a corvette and a brig.

Undaunted at this discovery, the British laid to in line of battle all night, and in the morning hoisted their colours, offering battle if the enemy chose to come down. About noon they seemed determined to make an attack, and endeavoured to cut off the retreat of the merchantmen; but the latter having stood towards them with a press of sail, and three of the vessels having opened their fire, the enemy steered away to the eastward, under all the sail they could set, and were pursued for upwards of two hours, when Captain Dance deemed it advisable, on account of the immense property at stake, to tack and proceed to the Straits of Malacca. On their arrival at Malacca, they were informed that the squadron they had engaged was that of Admiral Linois, con-

u 2

sisting

sisting of the Marengo, of 84 guns, the Belle Poule and Semillante, heavy frigates, a corvette of 28, and the Batavian brig William, of 18 guns.

It appears from the subsequent testimony of some English prisoners on board Linois's squadron, that when he saw the China fleet, he expressed his satisfaction to those captives; telling them it would prove a fortunate day for them, but a sorrowful one for their country; as it was his intention to give them *one* of the China ships, to carry them to Malacca; *seven* of the largest, he said, he should man and arm; and the *remainder* he was determined to sink!

Several other naval actions, though of smaller magnitude, took place this year, and added fresh laurels to the brows of our intrepid seamen. The ports of Dunkirk, Nieuport, Ostend, Trepont, Fecamp and Etaples, were now blockaded; and Havre suffered a severe bombardment, while the boastful enemy vainly continued to threaten an invasion of England. It is likewise necessary to observe, that the war in India proved highly honourable to the British arms, and occasioned a considerable augmentation of territory in that country.

France in the mean time continued to groan under the most tyrannic despotism; and acts of violence were committed by her government disgraceful to civilization and the

the feelings of human nature. Thus on pretence of a conspiracy against the First Consul, and the *liberties* of the republic, the amiable Duc d'Enghien was basely murdered at midnight, and buried in the garden of the castle of Vincennes; Pichegru, though reported to have *strangled himself* in prison, was believed to have been racked to death; nineteen were sentenced to suffer death and confiscation of their goods; five were doomed to two years imprisonment; five others were ordered to the police for correction, and eighteen were acquitted. Bonaparte thought fit to extend his *gracious* pardon to some of these persons: but general Moreau was driven into exile, and the heroic Georges suffered decapitation, exclaiming, at the last moment, *Vive le Roi! Vive Louis XVIII!*

Yet, notwithstanding these dreadful acts of violence and tyranny, to which may be added an attempt to poison Louis XVIII. the base seizure and imprisonment of Sir Thomas Rumbold, and the *robbery* of Mr. Wagstaffe, messenger to the court of Petersburg; in the course of this year, 1804, Bonaparte found means to assume an imperial diadem, and the pope was compelled to sanction the coronation ceremony with his presence and benediction; the trees of liberty were pulled up by the new emperor's command, in all parts of Paris and its environs; and the red cap of liberty was re-

moved

moved to make room for the imperial eagle!

As it was a known fact that the court of Spain had long furnished the French government with considerable quantities of money, and as even some of her naval preparations seemed calculated to excite suspicion, the British ministry demanded such satisfaction as might preserve the amity subsisting between the two countries. But, as, after a long and protracted negociation, no satisfactory answer could be obtained, it was deemed requisite to resort to more strenuous measures, and orders were accordingly issued for the detention of Spanish vessels till the subject under consideration should be finally arranged.

On the 2d of October, Captain Moore discovered four large Spanish ships steering towards Cadiz, the van ship carrying a broad pennant, and the ship next her a rear-admiral's flag. After hailing to make them shorten sail, a shot was fired, and a message sent to the rear admiral, informing him of Captain Moore's orders to detain his squadron, and expressing an earnest desire to avoid any effusion of blood. An engagement, however, immediately took place, in which three of the Spanish vessels were taken, and a fourth (La Mercedes, of 36 guns and 280 men,) unfortunately blew up; and, excepting 40
taken

taken up by the Amphion's boats, all on board perished.

On the 14th of December, the Spanish declaration of war against his Britannic majesty was published at Madrid; and on the 11th of January, 1805, letters of marque and reprisal were issued out against Spain, and a copy of the manifesto was laid before parliament on the 15th instant.

In consequence of the tenth report of the commissioners appointed to enquire into naval abuse, &c. Mr. Whitbread brought forward a motion in the House of Commons, on the 8th of April, against Lord Melville, as having connived at a gross misapplication of the public money, by his agent, Mr. Trotter; and two days afterward, Mr. Pitt announced the resignation of the accused, as first lord of the admiralty.

On the 11th, a treaty of concert was concluded between Great Britain and Russia; and every probable mean was used to engage Austria in the confederacy; but that power, for the present, was completely overawed by the gigantic and rapidly increasing acquests of Bonaparte, whose coronation as king of Italy was solemnized at Milan on the 26th of the ensuing month.

On the 25th of June the motion for lord Melville's impeachment was carried in the House of Commons, after the subject had

been

been long and ably discussed by the contending parties.

The ensuing month vice admiral Sir R. Calder discovered the combined squadrons of France and Spain, which had hitherto eluded the utmost vigilance of the British cruisers: and notwithstanding his inferiority of force, and the extreme haziness of the weather, he succeeded, after an action of four hours, in capturing the San Rafael, of 84 guns, and the Firme, of 74. The fleets remained nearly in sight the two following days; and the conduct of the noble admiral in not renewing the engagement, has suffered professional censure; but his courage is allowed to be unimpeached.

Whilst preparations were making on the continent for curbing the lawless and boundless rapacity of the French, our immortal Nelson was anxiously seeking the enemy, but without effect. On the 19th of October, however, he received the gratifying intelligence that they had put to sea; and on the 21st they appeared in the vicinity of Cape Trafalgar, presenting a line of 33 ships, of which 18 were French, and the remaining 15 Spanish. The British hero had but 27 vessels under his command; yet he rushed with noble impetuosity to the conflict; caused his ship to be carried alongside his old acquaintance, the Santissima Trinidada, and engaged the combined forces at the

very

very muzzles of their guns. The conflict was severe and obstinate; but, about three o'clock P. M. many of the enemy's ships having struck, their line gave way, and victory soon decided in favour of our gallant countrymen. Admiral Gravina, with 10 ships, stood toward Cadiz, and some of the headmost ships in the van went off; leaving to his majesty's squadron 19 ships of the line (of which 2 were first rates) and 3 flag officers, viz. Admiral Villeneuve, the commander in chief; Don J. M. D'Avila, vice admiral; and the Spanish rear admiral, Don B. H. Cisneros. Thus the proud boast of France that she had " made a marine of 20,000 sailors," was annihilated at a blow; the vaunted labour of ten years was shaken to its foundation; and Bonaparte's pleasing visions of *ships, colonies,* and *commerce,* dissolved in air.

This brilliant victory, however, was dearly purchased, and the glories of the day were sadly overcast by the death of the gallant Lord Nelson, who received a musket ball in his left breast, about the middle of the action, and soon afterwards expired.

In the mean time, Austria had been induced to join the coalition against France, and a continental war had commenced, which at first gave rise to very sanguine conjectures. The command of the army in Germany, however, being unfortunately given

given to field marshal baron Mack,—a man by no means qualified to oppose the promptitude, energy, and sudden evolutions of Bonaparte; and the French having succeeded in bringing the Austrians to action before they could be joined by the forces from Russia, a series of disasters succeeded each other with the greatest rapidity. After the battles of Wertingen and Guntzburg, Ulm was surrendered; when 33,000 men marched out before a French division, and 3000 sick and wounded remained in the hospitals. The conquerors then pushed on to Vienna, and the citizens endured the mortification of being subject to a provisional government, while their lawful prince and his gallant adherents were compelled to retire towards Moravia. In Italy, the Austrians were equally unsuccessful; and the fatal battle of Austerlitz, in which 100 pieces of cannon and 45 standards were taken by the enemy, terminated the campaign and the war; an armistice being agreed on two days afterward, and a definitive treaty of peace concluded at Presburg on the 26th of December.

In India, the British arms had been exercised against Holkar, Scindiah, &c.; and our troops in some instances, sustained considerable loss; but the intrepidity and good fortune of general Lake at length triumphed over all difficulties; and in the month of

December,

December, treaties of peace and amity were concluded between the native princes and the British government.

On the 5th of January, 1806, upwards of 20,000 persons were admitted to see the remains of Lord Nelson lying in state in the painted chamber at Greenwich Hospital, which was entirely hung with black, and most judiciously lighted; a guard of volunteers and a great number of police officers were stationed to preserve order; but many accidents happened during this and the two following days, from the immense pressure of the populace. On the 8th the body was removed to Westminster in the state barge, attended by the lord mayor, aldermen, and a committee appointed by the corporation of London; minute guns firing, and the bells of the various churches tolling during the procession: and the ensuing day, the grand and impressive ceremony of interment took place at St. Paul's cathedral; the whole exhibiting the most splendid spectacle of the kind ever witnessed in this country; and evincing at once the gratitude and regret of an amiable prince and his beloved people.

The 23d was marked by the demise of that great statesman, the Right Hon. William Pitt, in consequence of extreme debility brought on by excessive anxiety and unremitting

unremitting attention to business; and the unfortunate issue of the war on the continent is supposed to have contributed largely to hasten his death. Four days afterward, the House of Commons decreed him a public funeral, which was accordingly solemnized, on the 22d of February, in Westminster Abbey.

Whilst these events occupied the public mind at home, the British arms proved successful on the coast of Africa, and the Cape of Good Hope was annexed to our conquests. The attack under General Sir D. Baird and Sir Home Popham was extremely gallant, and the terms of capitulation highly honourable to the British character.

An entire change now took place in the ministry, of which Lord Grenville became the head. Lord Henry Petty filled the vacant office of Mr. Pitt, as chancellor of the exchequer; the Right Hon. Thomas Lord Erskine was appointed lord high chancellor of Great Britain; and the Right Hon. C. J. Fox took the place of Lord Mulgrave, as one of his majesty's principal secretaries of state.

The illiberal conduct of the Prussian cabinet, in seizing various parts of the electorate of Hanover, and excluding all British vessels from their ports, induced his majesty, on the 5th of April, to lay an embargo on all Prussian shipping within the united

united kingdom ; and measures were immediately taken for the blockade of the entrance of the rivers Ems, Weser, Elbe, and Trave ; and on the 21st, Lord Grenville announced to the House of Lords the recal of our minister from Berlin, and the necessity of adopting, provisionally, measures of just retaliation against the commerce and navigation of Prussia. Mr. Fox made a similar communication to the Commons, and an address to his majesty was unanimously voted on the occasion.

On the 29th of the same month commenced the ceremonial of the trial of Lord Melville in Westminster Hall, when Mr. Whitbread addressed the peers in a most nervous and eloquent speech of three hours and three quarters. However, on the seventeenth day of trial, the noble viscount was honourably acquitted by a majority of 686 voices. The dukes of York, Cumberland, Cambridge, and Gloucester, generally voted Not guilty; and the Dukes of Clarence, Kent, and Sussex, generally Guilty, except on the 4th article of impeachment, which totally fell to the ground.

On the 11th of June, Louis Bonaparte was proclaimed king of Holland at the Hague; his *august brother* having *generously* agreed to the *request* of their High Mightinesses, in a matter *so well adapted to secure the tranquillity* of Europe. The new monarch

narch, however, seems but little admired by his subjects, as he had been already compelled to *suppress* one of the Amsterdam papers, and to hold out *menaces* to those who presume to *talk lightly* of the government or its allies.

Early in the ensuing month, the fort and capital of Buenos Ayres in South America surréndered to a detachment of his majesty's troops under the command of major-general Beresford, assisted by Sir Home Popham; and on the 20th of September, the treasure taken from this settlement was brought, in eight waggons, to the Bank of England, where 1,086,203 dollars, and a box filled with jewels and precious stones, were deposited; the field-pieces and colours taken on the same occasion were carried to the Tower.

The month of September was also marked by the news of some successful battles which took place early in July in Sicily; particularly that of Maida, in which the French army sustained a signal defeat by the troops under the command of Gen. Stuart. Upwards of 700 of the enemy were buried upon the field; and the prisoners, among whom were several officers, amounted to above a thousand. About a thousand more, in different parts, also notified their readiness to surrender. " In short," says the General in his dispatches, " never has
the

the pride of our presumptuous enemy been more severely humbled, nor the superiority of British troops more gloriously proved than in the events of this memorable day." This decisive victory was soon followed by the surrender of Cotrone, with all its stores, magazines, &c. and the total evacuation of Calabria Ultra, in which single province, previous to the battle of Maida, the enemy had a distributed force of at least 9000 men. Gaeta, the castle of Amantea, and other places, likewise surrendered to the British arms; and our brave countrymen were received with enthusiasm, as the deliverers of an oppressed people.

The severe indisposition of Mr. Fox, which had for some time precluded his attention to business, terminated in his dissolution on the 13th of September; and on the 10th of the following month, his remains were conveyed with great pomp and solemnity to Westminster Abbey, where they were deposited within eighteen inches of the grave of the late illustrious W. Pitt, and immediately adjoining the monument of the great Lord Chatham. Fifteen days after this ceremony, the imperial parliament was dissolved, and writs issued for a new parliament to be assembled on the 15th of December.

Notwithstanding the infatuation which had so long blinded the court of Prussia to

its

its true interests, the augmenting and inordinate pretensions of France drove it at length to adopt that determination of resistance, which ought to have contributed to the success of the late coalition. An accommodation, of course, took place with his Britannic majesty; pamphlets were distributed among the Prussian troops, inviting them to preserve their ancient glory; rewards and honours were liberally promised to all who should signalize their courage and loyalty; and every probable mean was used to ensure success. In the first operations, the French obtained some trifling success; but soon afterward, an important action took place, in which the French were defeated with the loss of 6,000 killed, and 14,000 taken prisoners. On subsequent occasions, however, the Prussian army sustained the most dreadful reverses: the battles of Jena and Auerstadt were productive of the most distressing consequences: whole armies, and strong fortresses, either from panic or treachery, surrendered without a blow; and the capital itself was abandoned to the insulting conqueror, who now resolved to push his victories into Poland.

In the month of March, by the influence of Bonaparte's advice, or *mandate*, the Grand Signior declared war against Russia and England, and English residents and property were immediately seized; and the

conduct

conduct of the Ottoman court was soon imitated by the deys of Algiers and Tripoli. The Servians, however, who had been expected to assist the Turks, took part with the Russians, and the latter severely injured the enemy by their blockade of all the ports in the Ionian and Egean seas; while a British fleet passed the Dardanelles with a view to destroy the Turkish marine.

During these occurrences abroad, his Britannic majesty had an opportunity of demonstrating his warm and pious attachment to the protestant religion, as established in his dominions; and this opportunity he embraced in a manner which will reflect lustre upon his crown and character to succeeding generations. The bill commonly called the "Catholic Bill" having for its object the emancipation of papists from their present inability to hold places of trust, &c. &c. in the British government, had been brought into parliament; and supported with the utmost force of argument by the then ministers; although they were perfectly aware that his majesty, from a conscientious adherence to his coronation oath, the established religion of his church, and the safety and happiness of his protestant subjects, would never consent to its passing into a law. His majesty therefore demanded a solemn pledge, that, in case of their continuing in office, they should make no new

x 3

attempt

attempt of a similar nature. This demand, though founded on the best and purest reasons, was peremptorily rejected; and our gracious sovereign, with a firmness worthy of his title as "defender of the faith," dismissed his ministers, and placed at the head of the new administration, the Duke of Portland, as first lord of the treasury: the Right Hon. Spencer Perceval, as chancellor of the exchequer; and the Right Hon. Lord Eldon, as lord chancellor. This month was also marked by an act for the abolition of the slave trade—that nefarious and abominable traffic which had so long tarnished the glory of a *free* country, and lacerated every humane bosom with the most poignant feelings and the deepest regret.

On the continent, appearances were for some time favourable to the allies; and it was generally supposed that the laurels which Buonaparte had gathered in Italy and Germany, were destined to wither in the morasses of Poland. The Russians, animated by the presence and intrepidity of their emperor, occasionally performed prodigies of valour, and the French troops were compelled to retreat before them with considerable loss. The surrender of Dantzic, however, on the 26th of May, seems to have completely changed the aspect of affairs: the eagle of victory again perched on the French standards; and subsequent to

the

the battle of Friedland, which seems to have been nearly as dreadful and as unfortunate to the allies, as those of Marengo, Austerlitz, and Jena, the victorious forces obtained easy possession of Koningsberg, where they are said to have found several hundred thousand quintals of corn, together with all the warlike stores sent from England, and a hundred and sixty thousand muskets, not unpacked!

These successes on the part of the enemy seem to have determined the Emperor of Russia against the continuance of the war; and, strange to relate! the two hostile leaders, Alexander and Napoleon, were seen *embracing* each other at their conference on the Niemen so early as the 24th of June. The king of Prussia, now no longer supported by Russia, was compelled to submit to his hard destiny; and a peace was concluded at Tilsit, by which the Prussian monarchy has been diminished nearly one half, and Russia has been rounded by territory containing a population of 200,000 souls!

At home, the violent opposition against his majesty's ministers rendered the disssolution of parliament expedient; and writs were issued for a new one, which was opened by commission on the 26th of June.

In the following month an action took place between the Leopard and the Ameri-

can

can frigate Chesapeak, which appeared. likely to produce a serious misunderstanding between Great Britain and the United States. The Chesapeak was known to have several deserters from the British service on board ; and though representations of the fact were made to the American secretary, no satisfactory answer was given. On the Chesapeak sailing for the Mediterranean, therefore, the captain of the Leopard was ordered to examine her for deserters, and on the search being peremptorily refused, an action commenced, in which the Americans had 6 men killed and 21 wounded.

In consequence of this occurrence, the inhabitants of Norfolk, and other parts of America, entered into some violent resolutions ; and Mr. Jefferson thought proper to publish a proclamation, prohibiting all intercourse with our ships, and all supplies of water and provisions. Great numbers of privateers were also proposed to be fitted out at Baltimore, New York, Philadelphia, &c. But, from more recent accounts, it is to be hoped this unpleasant business will be amicably adjusted.

On the 4th of August, after a rather uninteresting session, the parliament was prorogued by commission, when the following appropriate remarks were delivered in his majesty's name :

" The immense extension of the power

and

and influence of France, and the undis-
guised determination of the enemy to employ the means and resources of those countries which he possesses or controuls, for
the purpose of effecting the ruin of his majesty's kingdom, undoubtedly present a formidable view of the difficulties and dangers
which this country has to encounter. But
his majesty trusts that the loyal and brave
people over whom he reigns, are not to be
daunted or disheartened. From the recollection of those difficulties under which his
people have successfully struggled, and of
those dangers which they have happily surmounted, his majesty derives the consolation of believing that the same spirit and
perseverance which have hitherto remained
unbroken, will continue to be exerted with
unabated vigor and success."

Consistent with the principles expressed
in this speech, the British ministry, understanding that Bonaparte designed to turn
the naval force of Denmark against us, sent
out an expedition, under lord Cathcart and
admiral Gambier, in order to attack Copenhagen, and to obtain possession of the
Danish fleet. This enterprize proved completely successful, being terminated on the
7th of September, by the capitulation of the
town and citadel, after a bombardment of
several days, and the surrender of the whole
of the fleet, consisting of 18 ships of the line,
14 frigates, 6 brigs, and 25 gun-boats.

Shortly after the conclusion of the treaty of Tilsit, the restless and ambitious Corsican meditated the complete subversion of the Spanish monarchy, and resolved to erect on its ruins a splendid establishment for a branch of his own family. Accordingly, he contrived, under a variety of specious pretences, to introduce a powerful body of his troops into Spain; he then induced the reigning monarch to make a formal renunciation of his crown; and having dexterously allured his successor, Ferdinand, beyond the protection of an army who would probably have shed the last drop of their blood in his defence, he sent him a prisoner to France, and bestowed the sovereignty of Spain and of the Indies on his own brother Joseph.

An outrage so daring and unexampled naturally produced a general consternation among the deluded Spaniards; but no sooner had this universal panic subsided, than they broke out into open insurrection, and, in the first ebullitions of their rage and resentment, vowed eternal war against their base and unprincipled oppressors. The French troops were consequently defeated in various parts; and king Joseph, with his valiant army, were compelled to retire from Madrid with the most disgraceful precipitation. Juntas, both supreme and central, were also formed; war was declared against France, in the name of Ferdinand the Seventh; and deputies were

dispatched

dispatched to solicit the assistance of the British government, with which peace had been already proclaimed. This application was immediately attended to; an expedition was fitted out, under the command of Sir David Baird; and liberal supplies of arms, ammunition, and money were sent to the patriotic Spaniards.

The successes, however, which had for some time crowned the arms of justice, soon reverted to the standards of oppression; for Bonaparte, with that promptitude which forms so distinguishing a trait in his character, reappeared on the frontiers of Spain, with a numerous army; and, in a series of engagements, vanquished the patriots, regained all the strong places which they had wrested from his myrmidons, and triumphantly entered the ill-fated capital.

The prince regent of Portugal, who, under British protection, had emigrated with his court to the Brazils, addressed a spirited manifesto to his subjects, which produced a considerable sensation in the north of Portugal, and led to the expulsion of the French forces, who had invaded that part of the country. The Portuguese juntas which were formed on this occasion solicited the aid of Great Britain; and a numerous force, under sir Arthur Wellesley, was sent over to attack the enemy's army under General Junot. After some skirmishes, a severe and obstinately

nately contested battle was fought near the village of Vimiera; and such was the effect of British valour on this occasion, that the French were compelled to retreat, with the loss of thirteen pieces of cannon, and about 3000 men in killed and wounded. On the following day, however, sir Hugh Dalrymple, who had been sent from Gibraltar to take the command of all the British corps in Portugal, arrived at Cintra, the place which the conquerors had occupied after the battle; and, a few hours after his arrival, Junot sent in a flag of truce, proposing a cessation of hostilities. This was readily granted; and a convention was soon afterwards concluded between the two generals, by which the French army was to evacuate Portugal, on condition of being conveyed to France at the expence of the British. One article, however, which stipulated that the Russian fleet, then lying in the Tagus, should either remain there unmolested, or return home, was peremptorily rejected by sir C. Cotton, to whom it was subsequently surrendered, on condition of being restored six months after the conclusion of peace between Russia and Great Britain. The convention of Cintra excited the greatest dissatisfaction in England, and petitions poured in from all parts of the kingdom, calling loudly for an enquiry into that unaccountable transaction. A formal declaration of his majesty's disapproval of

both

both the armistice and the convention was officially communicated to Sir H. Dalrymple; and a court of enquiry was instituted, but without producing any thing worthy of notice.

The commencement of the year 1809 was marked by an event equally glorious and disastrous to the British forces in Spain. Sir John Moore, who, with the troops under his command, had penetrated almost to the centre of the kingdom, was compelled, by the overwhelming numbers of the French, to retreat with the utmost precipitation. On this occasion he displayed the most consummate skill, and in the engagement which took place on his arrival at Corunna, the enemy were completely defeated, and compelled to fly in all directions; but whilst the British troops, literally covered with laurels, embarked on board their transports without molestation, they had to regret the loss of their heroic commander, who fell at the commencement of the battle.

The hope of ultimately succeeding against the tyrant of the continent had nearly subsided, when the Austrian cabinet published a declaration of war against France. Bonaparte, however, having contrived to force himself between the principal divisions of the Austrian army, defeated them in several engagements, and soon made himself master of Vienna; and notwithstanding a serious repulse

pulse which he received from the archduke Charles, on the bank of the Danube, the battle of Wagram was so decisive, that the emperor of Austria was obliged to request a cessation of hostilities, and subsequently to conclude a peace, upon very disadvantageous terms.

Whilst these occurrences were passing on the continent, the British cabinet hoped, by making a diversion in favor of the allies, to check the progress of the enemy. And Sir Arthur Wellesley, having again defeated the French troops, and chased them from Portugal, marched, with a numerous force, into Spain, and formed a junction with the Spanish army, commanded by general Cuesta, at Talavera. On the 27th of July an engagement took place, in which the French were compelled to retreat across the Alberche, with the loss of twenty pieces of cannon, a considerable quantity of ammunition, and nearly ten thousand men in killed and wounded. But as the British general received intelligence, soon after the battle, that the enemy designed to attack him both in front and in rear with a very superior force, he immediately recrossed the Tagus, and retreated to a strong position in Portugal. It must be added, that the heroic bravery exhibited by sir Arthur, in the battle of Talavera, induced his Britannic majesty to create him a peer, by the title of viscount Wellington.

With

With a view to occasion a further diversion on behalf of the Austrians, and also to attempt the capture or destruction of the French vessels lying in the Scheldt, a British army of fifty thousand men was landed on the island of Walcheren; but a considerable time having elapsed prior to the reduction of Flushing, the enemy collected a numerous force, raised several formidable batteries, and conveyed their ships up the river beyond fort Lillo. That part of the country, also, where the English might have landed was completely inundated. Walcheren, the only fruit of this expensive and unfortunate expedition, was to have been retained by the conquerors, for the purpose of shutting up the mouth of the Scheldt, and of facilitating the introduction of British manufactures into Holland. This design, however, was rendered abortive by the unhealthiness of the climate; and after great numbers of the troops had fallen a sacrifice, the British army evacuated the island, on the 9th of December, having previously destroyed the fortifications, arsenal, docks, and basin. Some old ships, filled with stones, were also sunk at the entrance of the Scheldt, to preclude an escape of the French fleet from the place of its retreat.

The parliamentary proceedings of this year were rendered remarkable by an enquiry into the conduct of the duke of York, as commander in chief; in consequence of his hav-

ing

ing been charged with an illegal disposal of commissions in the army. His royal highness, though acquitted by a majority of the house of commons, resigned his office, in which he was succeeded by Sir David Dundas.

Among the gallant actions which were performed this year by the British navy, we must notice an attack upon the French fleet in Basque-roads, by lord Gambier and lord Cochrane, on the 11th and 12th of April; when one ship of 120 guns, five of 74, and two frigates, were driven on shore in such a situation as ensured their destruction; and one of 80, two of 74, one of 50 guns, and three frigates were burnt. And to this exploit must be added the capture of a Russian flotilla and convoy in the Baltic, by Sir J. Saumarez; the destruction of three sail of the line, two frigates, and twenty French transports, in the Bay of Rosas, by lord Collingwood; and the reduction of the islands of Cayenne, Martinique, Isch, and Prorida, and the city of St. Domingo.

Whilst these victories were extending the honours of the British arms abroad, the nation was exhilarated at home by the important and interesting event of their beloved monarch's entrance into the fiftieth year of his reign. It was accordingly celebrated as a jubilee by all ranks throughout the united kingdom. In the metropolis, the joyous day was

was announced by the ringing of bells, the display of flags, and the assembling of the various corps of regular and volunteer troops. The forenoon was devoted to public worship; collections and subscriptions were made for the relief of indigent families, and the emancipation of poor debtors; and the evening exhibited a splendid and general illumination.

The commencement of the year 1810 was marked by the entrance of the French into Andalusia, their manœuvres having completely deceived the Spaniards. On the 29th of January, they approached within two leagues of Seville, from which the inhabitants fled in all directions; and in consequence of the general alarm excited by this irruption, immense numbers sought an asylum within the walls of Cadiz. After some time, however, the general panic subsided, as little doubt was entertained of the safety of Cadiz, and a considerable supply of provisions arrived to supply the wants of the increased population. The Spanish fleet lying in the harbour was placed at the disposal of admiral Purvis; and both the military and political government of the fortress were entrusted to a mercantile junta, who were considered the most likely to adopt effectual measures for the public security. About the beginning of February the French entered Malaga, which was given up to the pillage of their troops for two days.

Almeida

Almeida surrendered to the army under Massena on the 27th of August; and Seville was reduced to the most wretched condition by the unremitting demands of the invaders, and the brutality of their general, Soult. The flame of patriotism, however, continued to spread among the Spaniards, whose desultory mode of warfare against their cruel enemy was, in many instances, crowned with success. And notwithstanding the pompous gasconades of the French with respect to Portugal, Lisbon remained secure beneath the shelter of the British arms, and the proud Massena thought proper to retreat before lord Wellington after the battle of Busaco.

Whilst these occurrences were taking place in Spain and Portugal, Louis Bonaparte, having in vain attempted to ameliorate the condition of the Hollanders, published a formal abdication of the crown; and on the 9th of July, this unfortunate country was annexed to France, by a decree of the Corsican tyrant, who, after divorcing his *empress* Josephine, had espoused the archduchess Maria Louisa, on the first of April!

At home, a considerable stir was occasioned, for a short time, by the punishment of sir Francis Burdett for a breach of privilege. On the 12th of March, this member made a motion, in the house of commons, respecting the recent committal of John Gale Jones, the conductor of a debating society,

for

for having announced, in a hand-bill, the following comparative question, " Which is
most deserving the censure of the public,—
Mr. Yorke's enforcement of the standing
order of the house to exclude strangers from
the enquiry into the Walcheren expedition,
or Mr. Windham's late attack on the liberty
of the press?" Sir Francis endeavoured to
prove, that though the house had a power of
committal over its own members, it had no
such power over others; but that this as-
sumption of authority was of very recent
date, and that it infringed upon the liberty of
the subject, as provided for by *magna charta*
and the bill of rights. His motion for the
liberation of Jones being negatived, he
thought proper to address a letter on the
subject to the electors of Westminster,
through the medium of Cobbett's Political
Register. This letter was brought forward
in the House of Commons by a Mr. Leth-
bridge, who moved that it was a libellous
and scandalous publication, and that sir F.
Burdett having acknowledged himself the
author, was guilty of a gross breach of the
privileges of parliament. After an adjourn-
ment of a week, these resolutions were carried, and a motion of sir R. Salisbury, that
sir Francis Burdett should be committed to
the Tower, was also carried by a majority of
37 members.

On the 6th of April, the baronet, who
had

had been apprised of these proceedings, came to town from Wimbledon; but, in an interview with the serjeant at arms, he urged the illegality of the speaker's warrant for his committal, and expressed his resolution to resist its execution, if necessary, by force. The reports which were immediately circulated inflamed the minds of the populace to such a degree, that a great number of the lower order of persons assembled before the baronet's house in Piccadilly, exclaiming " Burdett for ever!" and imprecating vengeance on his enemies. At night they paraded the streets, constraining the inhabitants to illuminate their houses, and breaking the windows of all who refused to comply with this demand. The appearance of a troop of horse-guards, together with Mr. Reid, the magistrate, and a number of constables, on the following day, excited the most alarming ferment in the multitude, which was now considerably augmented. Hisses, shrieks, groans, and every expression of indignation issued from all quarters; the guards were assaulted with showers of stones and brickbats; and even after the riot act had been read, the commotion was so great, that it became necessary to send to the Knightsbridge barracks for an additional body of cavalry, who galloped among the crowd, and drove them up and down Piccadilly, and into the adjoining

adjoining streets and alleys, where several persons were wounded, but only three seriously.

The following day, in consequence of the receipt of a letter from Sir F. Burdett, the sheriffs of Middlesex arrived in Piccadilly, attended by the *posse comitatûs*, who formed a guard in front of the baronet's house, while the horse guards, who had previously occupied that station, divided into two bodies, and took a position of about 500 yards on each side. The efforts of the sheriffs to appease the tumult, however, proved completely fruitless, and the horse guards were again under the necessity of dispersing the mob, sword in hand. At the same time considerable bodies of cavalry and infantry were marched to town, and pieces of artillery were planted in the park, and in each of the principal squares, to overawe the rioters.

At length, on the 9th of April, the officers, having forced an entrance through the kitchen window, the baronet was taken, and conveyed in a glass coach to the Tower, under a strong guard. The indignation of the multitude was now particularly directed against the soldiery; who, on their return from the Tower, were assaulted so furiously that they charged their assailants, and continued firing their carbines all the way through Fenchurch street, where a ball entering a shop, mortally wounded a corn porter of the name of Ebrall. After his death coroner's

inquests

inquests were held on him, and on the body of another person who had been shot in Piccadilly; and verdicts were returned of " wilful murder by life-guardsmen unknown." An inquest was also held on a third person, but, as he was proved to have attacked the military, the verdict returned was "justifiable homicide." At the prorogation of parliament, on the 21st of June, Sir Francis was liberated from the Tower, and great preparations had been made by his partisans to conduct him home in a triumphant procession; but this honour he declined, and retired, with the utmost privacy, to his seat at Wimbledon.

Another circumstance which excited a considerable degree of attention this year, was a most daring attempt upon the life of his royal highness the duke of Cumberland. About half past two o'clock in the morning of the 31st of May, the prince was roused out of his sleep, in his apartment at St. James's Palace, by two violent blows and cuts on the head. He at first supposed a bat was beating about his head; but a third wound convinced him of the contrary. He then leaped out of bed, and on receiving several other blows, retired to a small room adjoining his chamber; but the assassin followed, and wounded him across the thighs. His royal highness being unable to find his alarm bells, called Neale, his valet in waiting, who hastened to his master's assistance, and

alarmed

alarmed the house. Soon afterwards the duke went to the porter's room, and ordered Neale to awaken Salis, a Piedmontese valet. No answer being returned to Neale's repeated calls, the door of the bed room was forced open, and Salis was found lifeless on the bed, with his throat cut from ear to ear. It seems that this wretch (for he was evidently the assassin) having failed in completing his execrable design, had retired on the first alarm, and terminated his own existence. His coat, which was folded up in a chair, was stained with blood; a pair of his slippers and the sheath of the sabre with which he had attacked his master, were found in a closet adjoining the duke's chamber; and the blood left by his arm on one side of the narrow door, discovered the way by which he escaped. Fortunately, however, though the duke had received six different wounds, one upon the upper part of the forehead, a second down the cheek, a third upon the arm, a fourth, by which the little finger was almost severed from the hand, a fifth on the front of the body, and a sixth on the thigh, none of them proved mortal. His royal highness, as might have been expected, was confined for some time; but at length the public were gratified with an assurance of his perfect recovery.

This, however, was not the only calamity which befel the royal family of England during

during the year 1810. The amiable princess Amelia, his majesty's youngest daughter, after enduring a most tedious illness, and expecting, in vain, the renovation of her health, conceived a wish of presenting her royal father with some token of filial affection, previous to that awful change which she considered to be drawing very near. Accordingly, in an interview with his majesty, she placed on his finger a ring, which had been made for the purpose; but the affecting manner in which she performed this action, accompanied by the impressive words " *Remember me,*" proved too much for the agitated monarch, already weakened by many severe trials; and the indisposition, both bodily and mental, which ensued, involved the nation in sorrow, and rendered it necessary that parliament should turn their attention to the subject of a regency.—The princess, who had most unintentionally given this shock to the susceptible mind of her august parent, expired on the 2d of November, and was interred at Windsor.

From motives of delicacy, some time was suffered to elapse, before any decisive measures were adopted by parliament; and after repeated adjournments it was deemed advisable to proceed by bill rather than by address. Accordingly, at the commencement of the year 1811, a regency bill was prepared, and passed through both Houses of Parliament;

by

by which it was enacted that his royal highness the prince of Wales should exercise the
office and authority of regent of the united
kingdom of England and Ireland, in the
name and on the behalf of his majesty, during
the continuance of the indisposition which
had rendered this measure necessary. But
as the recovery of the sovereign was still con-
templated as a probable circumstance, it was
enacted that the power of conferring any title
of nobility should be suspended for twelve
months; and that all offices and pensions
which might be granted by the prince of
Wales should continue only during his regency, unless subsequently approved and ratified
by his august parent. The care of the royal
person was also committed to her majesty.

On the 27th of January the prince was regularly qualified for entering upon the high
office committed to him, by attending divine
worship and receiving the sacrament, at the
chapel royal St. James's, and the 6th of the
following month was appointed for swearing
him in, as regent of the united kingdom.

On this occasion all the royal dukes and a
numerous assemblage of privy counsellors met
at Carlton-house. The whole of the state
apartments were thrown open, and the illustrious characters present were ushered into an
apartment which, from the stile of its orna-
ments, has received the name of the *gold
room.* After the return of the summons, &c.

z   had

had been officially communicated to his royal highness, he approached in grand procession, preceded by the officers of his council. They passed through the room where the privy counsellors were assembled, and through the circular drawing room, into the grand saloon, a most sumptuous apartment in scarlet drapery, adorned with portraits of all the most celebrated admirals, whose brilliant exploits, under Divine Providence, have confirmed to the British isles their dominion over the sea. Here the prince took his seat at the head of the table; his royal brothers and cousin seating themselves on his right and left hand, according to their seniority; whilst all the officers of the household who were not privy counsellors ranged themselves on each side of the entrance to the saloon.

His royal highness having intimated his readiness to take the oaths, and to make the declaration prescribed by the regency act, the lord privy seal respectfully approached, and read, from a parchment, the following oaths, which the prince repeated with an audible voice.

" I do sincerely promise and swear that I will be true and faithful, and bear true allegiance to his majesty, king George. So help me God.

" I do solemnly promise and swear that I will truly and faithfully execute the office of regent of the united kingdom of Great Britain

tain and Ireland, according to an act of parliament passed in the 51st year of the reign
of his majesty king George the Third, intituled, An Act, &c. and that I will administer,
according to law, the power and authority
vested in me by virtue of the said act; and
that I will, in all things, to the utmost of my
power and ability, consult and maintain the
safety, honor, and dignity of his majesty, and
the welfare of his people. So help me God."

The regent having subscribed these oaths,
and also the declaration mentioned in an act
made in the 30th year of Charles II. intituled,
" An act for the more effectual preserving the
king's person and government, by disabling
papists from sitting in either house of parliament," the lord president had the honor to
kiss his hand. The royal dukes followed,
and afterwards the archbishop of Canterbury;
all the rest advanced to the chair, on both
sides, in the order in which they had been
seated at the table. The ceremony being
closed, a short levee was held in the drawing-
room, and an audience was afterwards given
to Mr. Perceval, who had again the honor of
kissing the regent's hand, as first lord of the
treasury, and chancellor of the exchequer.

Parliament was opened, by commission, on
the 12th of February; and in the speech
delivered on that occasion, a cheerful picture
was drawn of the skill and valour of our
forces in the late campaign, of the disappoint-

ment

ment of the enemy's plans in Spain and Portugal, and of the animation infused into his majesty's allies by the recent examples of British intrepidity. It was also stated that discussions were depending between England and America, which the regent earnestly desired to bring to an amicable conclusion; and the fullest confidence was expressed that the supplies of a zealous and liberal parliament would be found commensurate with the wants of government.

To this speech an address, as usual, was moved and carried. And on the 21st of February Mr. Perceval stated, in the House of Commons, that having during the discussions on the regency bill, expressed his intention of moving for a provision with respect to the regent's household, not to exceed 12 or 13,000l. he had submitted his plan to the prince; but his royal highness had declared he would not, for his own personal magnificence, add another burden to those already imposed upon the public. Mr. Perceval added, it was sufficiently obvious from the known character of the regent, that he had submitted to this instance of self-denial, and had refused all personal state from an economical consideration for the people; a consideration which would throw around him more real splendor than any regal establishment whatsoever.

But few bills of an interesting nature were
passed

passed during this session, except a bill for preventing vexatious arrests by raising the sum for which persons may be held to bail in mesne process ; an act for permitting the interchange of the British and Irish militias from their respective countries ; and a bill for preventing guineas, half guineas, and seven shilling pieces, from being taken for more than 21s. 10s. 6d. and 7s. respectively, and for preventing bank notes from being taken for less than the sums expressed in them. On the 24th of July, parliament was prorogued, by commission, to the 12th of November ; and on that day it was further prorogued to the 7th of January ensuing.

On the continent various successes attended the arms of the Spaniards and Portuguese and those of their cruel invaders ; but generally speaking, whenever the British forces engaged, Bonaparte had the mortification to discover that his legions were not *invincible ;* and some victories were obtained which will probably never be obliterated from the recollection of Britons, or of the patriotic bands on whose behalf they were achieved.

The battle of Barossa, which took place on the 5th of March, was fought under such peculiar circumstances and with such disparity of numbers, that lieutenant-general Graham, in his dispatches to the earl of Liverpool, begs leave to make a particular statement, in order to justify himself from the imputation

z 3

of

of *rashness* in his attempt. From this statement it appears that, after a nocturnal march of sixteen hours from the camp near Veger, the allied army arrived in the morning on the low ridge of Barossa, about four miles to the southward of the Santi Petri river. This height extends inland about a mile and a half, containing on the north the extensive healthy plain of Chiclana. A large forest of pines skirts the plain, and circles round the height at some distance, terminating down to the Santi. Petri ; the intermediate space between the forest and the north side of the height being uneven and broken. A well conducted attack on the rear of the enemy's lines by the van-guard of the Spanish army, having opened a communication with the Isle de Leon, Gen. Graham received directions to move down from the position of Barossa to that of the Torre de Bermesa, about half way to the Santi Petri, in order to secure the communication across that river, over which a bridge had been recently erected. This latter position occupies a narrow woody ridge, the right on the sea cliff, the left falling down to the Almanza creek, on the edge of the marsh ; while a hard sandy beach affords an easy communication between the western points of these two positions. Gen. Graham's division having halted on the eastern slope of the Barossa height, was marched, about 12 o'clock, through the wood towards the Bermesa,

mesa, cavalry patroles having previously proceeded towards Chiclana, without discovering
the enemy.   On the march intelligence was
received that the enemy had appeared in force
on the plain, and was advancing towards the
heights of Barossa. As that position was,
in reality, the key of that of Santi Petri,
Gen. Graham immediately countermarched,
in order to support the troops left for its defence, and this manœuvre was executed with
the greatest alacrity. It was impossible, however, on such difficult ground, to preserve
order in the columns, and there was never
time to restore it completely. But before
the troops could get entirely disentangled
from the wood, those on the Barossa height
were seen returning from it; while the enemy's left wing was rapidly ascending, his
right standing on the plain, at the edge of the
wood, within cannon shot. As a retreat,
under these circumstances, might have proved
extremely detrimental to the whole allied
army, an immediate attack was determined
on, notwithstanding the numbers and position
of the foe. As soon as the infantry was
hastily collected together, a battery of ten
guns opened and kept up a most destructive
fire in the centre; while the right wing proceeded to the attack of Gen. Rufin's division on the hill and drove them from their
position ; and the left wing decided the defeat of the division under Gen. Laval. A
reserve

reserve formed beyond the narrow valley; across which the enemy was closely pursued, shared the same fate; and in less than an hour and a half from the commencement of the action, the whole of the enemy's troops were in full retreat. In this brilliant affair the French are supposed to have lost about three thousand, in killed, wounded, and missing; and ten eagles and six pieces of cannon fell into the hands of the conquerors. Generals Rufin, Rosseau, and Bellegrade were also taken prisoners; the former of whom was wounded, and the second died soon after the engagement.

It may be proper to add, that when the expedition against the rear of the enemy was planned, an arrangement was made with Sir R. G. Keats, for an attack on the French batteries in Cadiz Bay, in order to effect a division. This plan, however, could not be executed, on account of the unfavourable weather, till the day after the battle of Barossa, when it was carried into effect with all the coolness and intrepidity of British seamen. All the batteries on the east side of the Bay, from Rota to St. Mary's, with the exception of Fort Catalini, were carried by storm, the guns spiked, and the works completely destroyed.

Another brilliant display of British valour and intrepidity occurred in the battle of Albuera, which took place between Marshal Soult

Soult and Marshal Sir H. Beresford on the 16th of June.

On the 12th it was reported that Soult had broken up from Seville, and had advanced towards Estremadura, notwithstanding the rumours which had been previously circulated that he was wholly engaged in strengthening the outworks of Seville, and that all his actions indicated a design of remaining on the defensive in Andalusia. On the receipt of this intelligence, Sir W. Beresford raised the siege of Badajoz, without sustaining any loss ; and having assembled the forces under his command, formed a junction, on the 15th, with generals Blake and Castaños, at Albuera. Next day he was attacked by the enemy, over whom the eagle of victory appeared for some time to hover, in consequence of the great superiority of his cavalry, and a numerous and heavy artillery. At length, however, the inflexible bravery of the British troops turned the balance in favor of the allies ; and in the night of the 17th the French were obliged to retire across the river, leaving about two thousand dead in the field of battle, and from nine hundred to a thousand taken prisoners. The losses sustained by the victors were also extremely great ; but the gallant commander remarks in his dispatches to Lord Wellington, " It is impossible to enumerate every instance of discipline and valour shewn on this severely contested

day ;

day ; but never were troops that more va-
liantly or more gloriously maintained the
honour of their respective countries. Every
individual most nobly did his duty ; and it
was observed that our dead, particularly the
57th regiment, were lying as they had fought
in ranks, and every wound was in front."—
It appears, indeed, that prodigies of valour
were shewn by the English and their allies on
this occasion, and that instances of *individual*
heroism were particularly conspicuous ; in
proof of which it may be interesting to sub-
join the following particulars related in the
House of Commons by the chancellor of the
exchequer. In the hottest of the engagement
an ensign of the name of Thompson was
called upon to surrender the colours which he
held ; but he resolutely declared he would
never give them up but with his existence,
and he fell a victim to his patriotic bravery.
Another ensign, of the name of Walsh, having fallen on the field severely wounded, tore
his colours from the staff, and thrust them
into his bosom, where they were found after
his death, Sir W. Beresford was also attacked by one of the Polish cavalry, whom
he dismounted, with the view of saving his
life ; but as the man persisted in his first design, one of our dragoons flew to the assistance of his beloved commander, and killed
the assailant.

Of the other affairs of the peninsula our
limits

limits only permit us to remark, that, in consequence of the skilful and judicious conduct of Lord Wellington, and the cordial unanimity subsisting between the British and the Spanish and Portuguese commanders, the French, notwithstanding some occasional successes, found it impossible to carry into execution their late boastful promise of speedily crushing every appearance of rebellion; and the patriotic ardour of the natives received the strongest encouragement from the disappointments and the diminished reputation of the enemy.

Of the naval exploits which graced this year the most prominent were, the defeat of the French and Italian squadrons near the isle of Lissa; and the reduction of the islands of Banda, Ternate, and Java.

The combined squadrons alluded to, consisted of five frigates, one corvette, one brig, two schooners, one gun-boat, and one zebec, forming a total force of 272 guns, and 2,655 men; to which were opposed the British ships Amphion, Cerberus, Volage, and Active, carrying in all but 124 guns, and 879 men. On the 13th of March, an enemy's fleet having been discovered off the north-point of the island of Lissa, the action commenced by the British squadron firing on the headmost ships, as they came within range. After vainly endeavouring to break the line in two places, the enemy's vessels

endeavoured

endeavoured to place the British between two
fires; but in this attempt they were so warmly received, and rendered so unmanageable
that they went on shore, on the rocks of
Lissa, in the greatest confusion. The British line was then wore, to renew the action;
the Amphion not half a cable length from
shore, the remainder of the enemy's star-
board division passing under her stern, and
engaging her at leeward; whilst the lar-
board division got to windward, and engaged the Cerberus, Active, and Volage.
In this situation the action recommenced with
great fury; the British vessels being frequently exposed to a raking fire from the enemy. " Nothing, however," says Captain
Hoste, " could withstand the brave squadron I had the honour to command. The
Flora having struck her colours at twenty
minutes past 11 a. m. and the Bellona having
followed her example, the enemy to windward endeavoured to make off; but were followed up as close as the disabled state of his
majesty's ships would permit; and the Active and Cerberus were enabled at 3 p. m. to
compel the sternmost of them to surrender,
when the action ceased, leaving us in possession of the Corona of 44 guns, and the
Bellona of 32 guns (the French Commodore): the Favourite of 44 guns on shore,
where she soon blew up with a dreadful ex-
plosion; the corvette of the enemy making
all

all possible sail to the north-west, and two frigates crowding sail for the port of Lessina; the brig making off to the south-east; and the small craft flying in every direction."

The capture of the island of Banda, on the 9th of August, was also particularly honourable to the British arms. The attack was made on this settlement during a dark and squally night by somewhat less than 200 men, consisting of seamen and marines, and about forty of the Madras European regiment under the command of Captain Cole. A dark cloud with a fall of rain covered their landing within a hundred yards of a battery of ten guns, which was taken in the rear, and an officer and his guard were made prisoners though the enemy were at their guns with lighted matches, having discovered the approach of his Britannic majesty's vessels on the preceding day. At the approach of day-light the assailants procured a guide to conduct them to the walls of the castle of Belgica; and after leaving the guard in charge of the battery, the party made a rapid movement round the skirts of the town, where the bugle was sounding an alarm among the enemy. In twenty minutes scaling ladders were placed against the walls of the outer pentagon of Belgica; and the gallantry and celerity with which they were hauled up, after the outwork was carried, and placed for the attack of the inner work,

A A

under

under a sharp fire from the garrison, were truly astonishing. The enemy, after firing three guns, and keeping up an ineffectual discharge of musketry for about ten or fifteen minutes, fled in all directions, leaving their colonel-commandant and ten others dead, and two officers and thirty prisoners in the hands of the victors. The day now beaming on the British, discovered to them the fort of Nassau and the sea defences at their feet, and the enemy at their guns at the different ports. Admiral Drury then dispatched a flag of truce to the governor, demanding the immediate surrender of the fort, and promising to protect all private property. At sun rise the Dutch flag was hoisted in Nassau, and the sea-batteries opened a fire on one of the British vessels then approaching the harbour. But on a second flag of truce being sent to the governor, with a menace of storming the fort and laying the town in ashes if the colours were not instantly struck, an unqualified surrender was agreed on; and the British heroes found themselves in possession of the two forts, and several batteries, mounting 120 pieces of cannon, and defended by nearly 700 disciplined troops and the militia.

It is also necessary to add, that the island of Ternate, though so famous for the strength of its fortifications, and memorable for its defence in the last war against the English, was completely subjugated, in less than one day,

day, (the 29th of August,) by a very inconsiderable force. From official documents it appears that the place was defended by five hundred regular troops, with a very large proportion of officers and Europeans, aided by the marine department, the Dutch inhabitants and burghers, and the king of Ternate's forces, of whom 250 were in the field, and an equal number from the sultan of Tidore, and the adjacent islands in alliance with the Dutch. But such were the gallantry, coolness, and precision of the British, that nothing could ultimately withstand their arms.

After a short but arduous campaign, in the month of August, Batavia, the capital of the island of Java, was taken by the British troops under sir Samuel Auchmuty; the enemy's most formidable works were carried, and themselves driven from the kingdoms of Bantam and Jacatra; so that, as lord Minto observes in his dispatches to the directors of the East India company, " an empire which for two centuries has contributed greatly to the power, prosperity, and grandeur of one of the principal and most respected states of Europe, has been thus wrested from the short usurpation of the French government, added to the dominion of the British crown, and converted from a seat of hostile machination and commercial competition into an augmentation of British power and prosperity. For this

this signal and illustrious service, Great Britain is indebted to the truly British intrepidity
of as brave an army as ever did honour to our
country; to the professional skill and spirit
of their officers; and to the wisdom, decision, and firmness of the eminent man who
directed their courage, and led them to victory."

But whilst our British tars were gathering
a profusion of laurels, in different parts, an
unpleasant occurrence took place between one
of his majesty's vessels and a ship belonging
to the American government; which threatened nothing less, in its consequences, than
a war between those countries.

The particulars of the engagement are thus
related by Captain Bingham, of the Little
Belt:—" At half past three *p. m.* on the
16th of May, a strange sail, which had been
previously discovered, appeared inclined to
give chace, when I made the private signal,
which was not answered. At half-past six,
finding he gained considerably on us, and
clearly discerning the stars in his broad pennant, I thought proper to bring to, and hoist
the colours, that no mistake might arise, and
that he might see what we were. The ship
was therefore brought to, the colours hoisted,
the guns double-shotted, and every prepara-
tion made in case of a surprise. By his
manner of steering down, he evidently wished
to lay his ship in a position for raking,
                                    which

which I frustrated by wearing three times. On his coming within hail, about a quarter past eight, I hailed, and asked what ship it was? He repeated my question. I again hailed, and asked what ship it was? He again repeated my words, and fired a broadside, which I immediately returned. The action then became general, and continued so for three quarters of an hour, when he ceased firing, and appeared to be on fire about the main hatchway. I was then obliged to desist from firing, as, the ship falling off, no gun would bear, and I had no aftersail to keep her to: all the rigging and sails were cut to pieces, and not a brace or bowline left. He then asked what ship this was? and on being told, he asked if I had struck my colours? I answered no, and asked what ship that was? and, as plainly as I could understand, he answered the United States frigate.

"Next morning he bore up again, and sent a boat on board, with an officer, and a message from Commodore Rogers, to say that he lamented the unfortunate affair which had happened; and that, had he known our force was so inferior, he should not have fired at us. I asked his motive for having fired at all; and his reply was that we fired the first gun at him, but this was positively not the case. He offered me every assistance I should stand in need of, and submitted to

me

me that I had better put into one of the ports of the United States, which I immediately declined. By the manner in which he apologised, it appeared evident that had he fallen in with a British frigate, he would certainly have brought her to action: and what further confirms me in that opinion is, that his guns were not only loaded with round and grape shot, but with every scrap of iron that could possibly be collected."

Such is the statement of Captain Bingham, of whose veracity we have not the smallest doubt. Commodore Rogers, however, asserts positively that the Little Belt fired first, and that, circumstanced as he was, it was a duty incumbent on him to avenge the insult committed upon the American flag. This statement was also confirmed by all the witnesses whom he thought proper to bring forward when the subject underwent a full investigation, by the order of the American Government.

On the 7th of January, 1812, the sixth session of the present parliament was opened by commission. The speech delivered on that occasion expressed the deepest sorrow for the continuance of his majesty's disposition;—the regent's approbation of the conduct of the British officers and troops in Spain and Portugal;—his satisfaction with the reduction of the islands of Java, Bourbon, and Mauritius;—an assurance that concilia-
tory

tory measures were intended to be adopted toward America;—and a firm reliance on the liberality of parliament for the necessary supplies. To this speech an address was moved and carried in both houses as usual.

On the 18th of February the restrictions imposed on the prince of Wales ceased, according to the provisions of the regency act: and it was now confidently supposed, by a numerous party both in England and Ireland, that a complete change of administration would take place. This expectation, however, was disappointed; the regent having received into his favor and confidence those persons who, during his restricted regency, had administered the affairs of government to his satisfaction.—With the following remarks of his royal highness, addressed, in a letter, to his brother, the duke of York, we shall close our historical account.

" A new æra is now arrived, and I cannot but reflect with satisfaction on the events which have distinguished the short period of my restricted regency. Instead of suffering in the loss of any of her possessions, by the gigantic force which has been employed against them, Great Britain has added most important acquisitions to her empire. The national faith has been preserved inviolate to our allies, and if character is strength, as applied to a nation, the increased and increasing

creasing reputation of his majesty's arms will shew to the nations of the continent how much they may still achieve when animated by a glorious spirit of resistance to a foreign yoke. In the critical situation of the war in the peninsula, I shall be most anxious to avoid any measure that can lead my allies to suppose that I mean to depart from the present system. Perseverance can alone achieve the great object in question; and I cannot withhold my approbation from those who have honourably distinguished themselves in support of it. I have no predilections to indulge—no resentments to gratify—no objects to attain, but such as are common to the whole empire. If such is the leading principle of my conduct, (and I can appeal to the past, in evidence of what the future will be), I flatter myself I shall meet with the support of parliament, and of a candid and enlightened nation."

Remarkable Events in this Reign.

1763. Peace proclaimed between England, France, and Spain.

1765. General warrants declared illegal.

1768. Mr. Wilkes, though an outlaw, carried his election for Middlesex: but was afterward expelled the House of Commons, and committed to the King's Bench prison.

1771.

1771. Mr. Wilkes liberated from prison, elected an alderman, and afterwards raised to the mayoralty of London.

1775. Hostilities commenced in the American colonies.

—— Hostilities began between England, France, and Spain.

1780. Riots in London; and war commenced against Holland.

1783. A general peace.

1789. A great revolution in France.

1791. The constitution of Canada settled, and Louis XVI. of France deposed.

1792. The king of Sweden shot at a masquerade.

1793. The king and queen of France beheaded; and war commenced between France and Great Britain.

1794. A dreadful fire near Ratcliffe-cross, which consumed six hundred houses; and a signal victory obtained over the French fleet by Lord Howe.

1795. The prince of Wales married the princess Caroline of Brunswick.

1796. The princess of Wales brought to bed of a daughter. This year also the Dutch spice islands surrendered to the British forces; and general Washington resigned the presidence of America.

—— Eighteen millions sterling raised, by voluntary subscription, in 15 hours and 20 minutes.

1797.

1797. Victory obtained by earl St. Vincent over the Spaniards, and over the Dutch fleet by admiral Duncan.

1798. Dangerous conspiracy in Ireland. French fleet defeated near Egypt by lord Nelson.

1799. Capture of Seringapatam by general Harris.

1800. Wet docks began near the Isle of Dogs.

1801. Union with Ireland carried into effect, and the royal style and titles altered.

1802. A general peace.

1803. Colonel Despard and six of his associates executed for high treason. An insurrection in Ireland.

—— War renewed with France and Holland.

—— Bonaparte crowned emperor of the French.

—— Dollars issued by the Bank of England as silver tokens.

1805. War commenced between England and Spain.

1806. Public funerals of lord Nelson, Mr. Pitt, and Mr. Fox.

—— Louis Bonaparte proclaimed king of Holland.

—— Brilliant victories of the British troops in Sicily.

1807. Peace concluded between Russia, France, and Prussia.

1807.

1807. Copenhagen, and the Dutch fleet, surrendered to the arms of his Britannic majesty.

—— Serious rupture with America by the Leopard, British frigate, insisting on searching for deserters on board tne American frigate Chesapeak.

1808. Revolution in Spain occasioned by Bonaparte's placing his brother Joseph on the Spanish throne.

1809. Bonaparte defeated, on the banks of the Danube, by the Archduke Charles, after a dreadfully sanguine battle.

—— Grand Jubilee on our beloved monarch's entering the fiftieth year of his reign.

1810. Bonaparte divorces his empress Josephine, and marries the archduchess Maria Louisa of Austria.

—— A partial revolution in South America.

—— Reduction of the Isle of France by the arms of Great Britain.

—— Death of the princess Amelia, and illness of his Britannic majesty.

1811. The prince of Wales appointed regent of the United Kingdom of Great Britain and Ireland, under certain restrictions.

—— The French troops completely defeated in the battles of Barossa and Albuera.

—— Capture of the islands of Banda, Ternate, and Java, by the forces of his Britannic majesty.

1811. Unpleasant

1811. Unpleasant rencontre between the United States frigate and the Little Belt.

—— Splendid fete given by the prince regent at Carlton House.

1812. The regency restrictions taken off.

THE END.

Printed by E. Hemsted, Great New Street,
Gough Square.